A smarter, more secure America

COCHAIRS:
RICHARD L. ARMITAGE
JOSEPH S. NYE, JR.

CSIS | CENTER FOR STRATEGIC & INTERNATIONAL STUDIES

ABOUT CSIS

At a time of newly emerging global opportunities and challenges, the Center for Strategic and International Studies (CSIS) provides strategic insights and policy solutions to decisionmakers in government, international institutions, the private sector, and civil society. A bipartisan, independent, nonprofit organization headquartered in Washington, D.C., CSIS conducts research and analysis to develop policy initiatives that look into the future and anticipate change.

Founded by David M. Abshire and Admiral Arleigh Burke at the height of the Cold War, CSIS was dedicated to finding ways for America to sustain its prominence and prosperity as a force for good in the world. Since 1962, CSIS has grown to become one of the world's preeminent public policy institutions, with more than 200 full-time staff and a large network of affiliated scholars focused on defense and security, regional stability, and transnational challenges ranging from energy and climate to global development and economic integration.

Former U.S. senator Sam Nunn became chairman of the CSIS Board of Trustees in 1999, and John J. Hamre has led CSIS as its president and chief executive officer since April 2000.

CSIS COMMISSION ON SMART POWER
A smarter, more secure America

Cochairs

RICHARD L. ARMITAGE, president, Armitage International

JOSEPH S. NYE, JR., distinguished service professor, Harvard University

Commissioners

NANCY LANDON KASSEBAUM BAKER, former U.S. senator (R-KS)

FREDERICK D. BARTON, senior adviser and codirector, Post-Conflict Reconstruction Project, CSIS

CHARLES G. BOYD, president and CEO, Business Executives for National Security

HELENE D. GAYLE, president and CEO, CARE USA

ALLAN E. GOODMAN, president, Institute for International Education

MAURICE R. GREENBERG, chairman and CEO, C.V. Starr, Inc.

CHUCK HAGEL, U.S. senator (R-NE)

SYLVIA MATHEWS BURWELL, president, Global Development Program, Bill & Melinda Gates Foundation

BETTY MCCOLLUM, U.S. representative (D-MN)

SANDRA DAY O'CONNOR, retired Supreme Court justice

THOMAS R. PICKERING, former U.S. ambassador and vice chairman, Hills & Company

JACK REED, U.S. senator (D-RI)

DAVID M. RUBENSTEIN, cofounder and managing director, The Carlyle Group

GEORGE RUPP, president and CEO, International Rescue Committee

MAC THORNBERRY, U.S. representative (R-TX)

TERENCE A. TODMAN, retired career ambassador and former assistant secretary of state

ANTHONY C. ZINNI, former commander in chief, U.S. Central Command and executive vice president, DynCorp International

JOHN ZOGBY, president and CEO, Zogby International

CSIS does not take specific policy positions; accordingly, all views expressed herein should be understood to be solely those of the commission members or individual author(s).

© 2007 by the Center for Strategic and International Studies. All rights reserved.

ISBN 978-0-89206-510-3

Library of Congress Cataloging-in-Publication Data

CSIS Commission on Smart Power.
  CSIS Commission on Smart Power : a smarter, more secure America / cochairs, Richard L. Armitage, Joseph S. Nye, Jr.
      p. cm.
  Includes bibliographical references.
  ISBN 978-0-89206-510-3 (pbk. : alk. paper) 1. United States—Foreign relations—2001– 2. Power (Social sciences)—United States. 3. Economic assistance—United States. 4. Technical assistance—United States. 5. Military assistance—United States. I. Armitage, Richard Lee, 1945– II. Nye, Joseph S. III. Center for Strategic and International Studies (Washington, D.C.) IV. Title. V. Series.

JZ1480.A5C75 2007
  327.73—dc22   2007044184

Cover Photo:
iStockImages.com – Statue of Liberty, New York, NY
Inside:
AusAID.com – page 7: aid in Sudan. DefenseLink.com – page 13: CH-47 Chinook helicopter flies over Kabul, Afghanistan; page 65: Military Sealift Command hospital ship USNS Comfort off the coast of Port-au-Prince, Haiti. Fotolia.com – page 45: river as source of water; page 55: Shanghai; page 59: wind energy plant. Getty Images – pages 6: U.S. Special Forces assist training of Iraqi Army Units; page 21: George W. Bush meets with Vladimir Putin; page 32: flag carriers. IllinoisPhoto.com – page 20: Katrina refugees in the Houston Astrodome. iStockPhoto.com – page 22: Rio de Janeiro; page 23: Mumbai; page 37: UN disaster relief; page 51: foreign languages; page 56: foreign currency; page 57: Vatnojokull glacier, Iceland. Liz Lynch – pages 3, 9, 11, 19, 25, 29, 30, 33, 38, 43, 47, 50, 52, 53, 54, 57, 58, 61, 62, 66, 67: Smart Power commissioners. Ruth Fremson/Redux Pictures – page 26: China. Simon Ho – page 30: UN Security Council.

The CSIS Press
Center for Strategic and International Studies
1800 K Street, N.W., Washington, D.C. 20006
Tel: (202) 775-3119   Fax: (202) 775-3199
E-mail: books@CSIS.org   Web: www.csis.org

CONTENTS

Executive Summary	1
Foreword Restoring America's Inspirational Leadership By John J. Hamre	3
Introduction How America Can Become a Smarter Power By Richard L. Armitage and Joseph S. Nye, Jr.	5
Commission Report	15
Part I: Diagnosis: Waning Influence	17
Part II: A Smart Power Strategy	27

1. Alliances, Partnerships, and Institutions
        Rebuilding the foundation to
        address global challenges
	27

2. Global Development
        Developing a more unified approach,
        starting with public health
	37

3. Public Diplomacy
        Improving access to international
        knowledge and learning
	47

4. Economic Integration Increasing the benefits of trade for all people	53

5. Technology and Innovation
        Addressing climate change and
        energy insecurity
	57

Part III: Restoring Confidence in Government	61
Appendix	71
About the Commissioners	73
How the Commission Functioned	77
CSIS Contributors	79

EXECUTIVE SUMMARY

America's image and influence are in decline around the world. To maintain a leading role in global affairs, the United States must move from eliciting fear and anger to inspiring optimism and hope.

In 2006, CSIS launched a bipartisan Commission on Smart Power to develop a vision to guide America's global engagement. This report lays out the commission's findings and a discrete set of recommendations for how the next president of the United States, regardless of political party, can implement a *smart power* strategy.

The United States must become a smarter power by once again investing in the global good—providing things people and governments in all quarters of the world want but cannot attain in the absence of American leadership. By complementing U.S. military and economic might with greater investments in soft power, America can build the framework it needs to tackle tough global challenges.

Specifically, the United States should focus on five critical areas:

- Alliances, partnerships, and institutions: The United States must reinvigorate the alliances, partnerships, and institutions that serve our interests and help us to meet twenty-first century challenges.

- Global development: Elevating the role of development in U.S. foreign policy can help the United States align its own interests with the aspirations of people around the world.

- Public diplomacy: Bringing foreign populations to our side depends on building long-term, people-to-people relationships, particularly among youth.

- Economic integration: Continued engagement with the global economy is necessary for growth and prosperity, but the benefits of free trade must be expanded to include those left behind at home and abroad.

- Technology and innovation: Energy security and climate change require American leadership to help establish global consensus and develop innovative solutions.

Implementing a smart power strategy will require a strategic reassessment of how the U.S. government is organized, coordinated, and budgeted. The next president should consider a number of creative solutions to maximize the administration's ability to organize for success, including the appointment of senior personnel who could reach across agencies to better align strategy and resources.

FOREWORD | RESTORING AMERICA'S INSPIRATIONAL LEADERSHIP

By John J. Hamre

America is a country of big ideas and common sense. A big idea was saying that we would put a man on the moon. Common sense was knowing which complex tasks would achieve that goal and putting in place a structure to accomplish them. We have been fortunate as a nation that when the chips have been down, we have found leaders who possess the vision to see what the world could be and the good sense to know what it will take to get there.

The vision and determination of these great men and women have lifted up Americans and people all over the world in ways that few would have ever dreamed. The rest of the world continues to look to us for our unique blend of optimism and pragmatism.

We have all seen the poll numbers and know that much of the world today is not happy with American leadership. Even traditional allies have questioned American values and interests, wondering whether they are compatible with their own. We do not have to be loved, but we will never be able to accomplish our goals and keep Americans safe without mutual respect.

There is a moment of opportunity today for our political leaders to strike off on a big idea that balances a wiser internationalism with the desire for protection at home. Washington may be increasingly divided, but Americans are unified in wanting to improve their country's image in the world and their own potential for good. We see the same hunger in other countries for a more balanced American approach and revitalized American interest in a broader range of issues than just terrorism. And we hear everywhere that any serious problem in the world demands U.S. involvement.

Of course, we all know the challenges before us. The center of gravity in world affairs is shifting to Asia. The threat America faces from nuclear proliferation, terrorist organizations with global reach, and weak and reckless states cannot be easily contained and is unlikely to diminish in our lifetime. As the only global superpower, we must manage multiple crises simultaneously while regional competitors can focus their attention and efforts. A globalized world means that vectors of prosperity can quickly become vectors of insecurity.

Joseph S. Nye, Jr., John J. Hamre, and Richard L. Armitage

These challenges put a premium on strengthening capable states, alliances, partnerships, and institutions. In this complex and dynamic world of changing demands, we greatly benefit from having help in managing problems. But we can no longer afford to see the world through only a state's narrow perspective. Statehood can be a fiction that hides dangers lurking beneath. We need new strategies that allow us to contend with non-state actors and new capabilities to address faceless threats—like energy insecurity, global financial instability, climate change, pandemic disease—that know no borders. We need methods and institutions that can adapt to new sources of power and grievance almost certain to arise.

Military power is typically the bedrock of a nation's power. It is understandable that during a time of war we place primary emphasis on military might. But we have learned during the past five years that this is an inadequate basis for sustaining American power over time. America's power draws just as much from the size of its population and the strength of its economy as from the vitality of our civic culture and the excellence of our ideas. These other attributes of power become the more important dimensions.

A year ago, we approached two of our trustees—Joe Nye and Rich Armitage—to chair a CSIS Commission on Smart Power, with the goal of issuing a report one year before the 2008 elections. We imposed the deadline for two reasons. First, we still have a year with the Bush presidency wherein these important initiatives can be furthered. Second, looking ahead to the next presidency, we sought to place before candidates of both parties a set of ideas that would strengthen America's international standing.

This excellent commission has combined that essential American attribute—outlining a truly big idea and identifying practical, tangible actions that would help implement the idea. How does America become the welcomed world leader for a constructive international agenda for the twenty-first century? How do we restore the full spectrum of our national power? How do we become a smart power?

This report identifies a series of specific actions we recommend to set us on that path. CSIS's strength has always been its deep roots in Washington's defense and security establishment. The nature of security today is that we need to conceive of it more broadly than at any time before. As the commission's report rightly states, "Today's central question is not simply whether we are capturing or killing more terrorists than are being recruited and trained, but whether we are providing more opportunities than our enemies can destroy and whether we are addressing more grievances than they can record."

There is nothing weak about this approach. It is pragmatic, optimistic, and quite frankly, American. We were twice victims on 9/11. Initially we were victimized by the terrorists who flew airplanes into buildings and killed American citizens and foreigners resident in this country. But we victimized ourselves the second time by losing our national confidence and optimism. The values inherent in our Constitution, educational institutions, economic system, and role as respected leader on the world stage are too widely admired for emerging leaders abroad to turn away for good. By becoming a smarter power, we could bring them back sooner.

What is required, though, is not only leadership that will keep Americans safe from another attack, but leadership that can communicate to Americans and the world that the safety and prosperity of others matters to the United States. The Commission on Smart Power members have spoken to such a confident, inspiring, and practical vision. I am sure they will not be the last.

INTRODUCTION | HOW AMERICA CAN BECOME A SMARTER POWER

By Richard L. Armitage and Joseph S. Nye, Jr.

This report is about power and how America wields it in the world.

The United States has been at war for six years now. During this time, debates over the best use of American power have tended to focus almost exclusively on fighting in Iraq and on the struggle against terrorists and violent extremism. Do we have the strategy and tools to succeed? What would constitute victory? What role should our military play? These questions have defied easy answers and divided a weary but determined nation.

The war debates will continue into 2008 and beyond. This report, to the extent possible, seeks to replace the narrow lens focused on Iraq and terrorism with a broader one that looks at U.S. goals, strategies, and influence in today's world. What principles should guide U.S. foreign policy in the next administration?

Our view, and the collective view of this commission, is that the United States must become a smarter power by investing once again in the global good—providing things that people and governments in all quarters of the world want but cannot attain in the absence of American leadership. By complementing U.S. military and economic might with greater investments in its soft power, America can build the framework it needs to tackle tough global challenges.

> The goal of U.S. foreign policy should be to prolong and preserve American preeminence as an agent for good.

Specifically, the United States should focus on five critical areas:

- Alliances, partnerships, and institutions: Rebuilding the foundation to deal with global challenges;
- Global development: Developing a unified approach, starting with public health;
- Public diplomacy: Improving access to international knowledge and learning;
- Economic integration: Increasing the benefits of trade for all people;
- Technology and innovation: Addressing climate change and energy insecurity.

Investing in the global good is not charity. It is smart foreign policy. America's allies and friends look to it for ideas and solutions, not lectures.

The goal of U.S. foreign policy should be to prolong and preserve American preeminence as an agent for good. Achieving this goal is impossible without strong and willing allies and partners who can help the United States to determine and act on priorities.

America should have higher ambitions than being popular, but foreign opinion matters to U.S. decisionmaking. A good reputation fosters goodwill and brings acceptance for unpopular ventures. Helping other nations and individuals achieve their aspirations is the best way to strengthen America's reputation abroad.

This approach will require a shift in how the U.S. government thinks about security. We will always have our enemies, and we cannot abandon our coercive tools. Resetting the military after six years of war is of critical importance. But bolstering American soft power makes America stronger. The U.S. government must develop the means to grow its soft power and harness the dynamism found within civil society and the private sector.

We must build on America's traditional sources of strength in a principled and realistic fashion. With new energy and direction, the United States could use its great power for even greater purposes and, in the process, preserve American values and interests far into the future.

HARD AND SOFT POWER

Power is the ability to influence the behavior of others to get a desired outcome. Historically, power has been measured by such criteria as population size and territory, natural resources, economic strength, military force, and social stability.

Hard power enables countries to wield carrots and sticks to get what they want. The Pentagon's budget for FY2008 is more than $650 billion and growing, many times more than the nearest competitor. The United States has the world's largest economy, and more than a third of the top 500 global companies are American. There is no other global power, and yet American hard power does not always translate into influence.

The effectiveness of any power resource depends first on context. Sources of strength change over time. Despite American technological advances that have made weapons more precise, they have also become more destructive, thereby increasing the political and social costs of using military force. Modern communications technology has diminished the fog of war, but also heightened and atomized political consciousness. Trends such as these have made power less tangible and coercion less effective. Machiavelli said it was safer to be feared than to be loved. Today, in the global information age, it is better to be both.

Soft power is the ability to attract people to our side without coercion. Legitimacy is central to soft power. If a people or nation believes American objectives to be legitimate, we are more likely to persuade them to follow our lead without using threats and bribes. Legitimacy can also reduce opposition to—and the costs of—using hard power when the situation demands. Appealing to others' values, interests, and preferences can, in certain circumstances, replace the dependence on carrots and sticks. Cooperation is always a matter of degree, and it is profoundly influenced by attraction.

This is evident in the changing nature of conflict today, including in Iraq and against al Qaeda. In traditional conflict, once the enemy is vanquished militarily, he is likely to sue for peace. But many of the organizations against which we are fighting control no territory, hold few assets, and sprout new leaders for each one that is killed. Victory in the traditional sense is elusive.

Militaries are well suited to defeating states, but they are often poor instruments to fight ideas. Today, victory depends on attracting foreign populations to our side and helping them to build capable, democratic states. Soft power is essential to winning the peace. It is easier to

attract people to democracy than to coerce them to be democratic.

Since America rose on the world stage in the late nineteenth and early twentieth centuries, it has wielded a distinctive blend of hard and soft power. Despite nineteenth-century military adventures in the Western hemisphere and in the Philippines, the U.S. military has not been put in the service of building a colonial empire in the manner of European militaries. Particularly since World War II, America has sought to promote rules and order in a world in which life continues to be nasty, brutish, and short for the majority of inhabitants.

American sources of soft power are plentiful. Soft power is more than mere cultural power, although the appeal of Hollywood and American products can play a role in inspiring the dreams and desires of others. Sources include the political values and ideas enshrined in the Constitution and Bill of Rights, U.S. economic and educational systems, personal contacts and exchanges, and our somewhat reluctant participation and leadership in institutions that help shape the global agenda. One of the biggest sources of U.S. soft power is quite simply America's obvious success as a nation.

Not everyone looks forward to a more interconnected and tolerant world. These ideas can be threatening to those who consider their way of life to be under siege by the West. Those who feel this divide most strongly are often the very people who seek to fight America and its allies.

Yet every year the United States attracts more than four times the number of immigrants than any other country, and hundreds of thousands of foreign scholars and students as well. America's history as an immigrant nation is an important source of its soft power. There is an enormous strength and vitality in the American civic spirit of opportunity, tolerance, mutual respect, and shared commitment and in an economy that rewards innovation and hard work. For people everywhere, the United States can be a partner for a better life.

WHAT IS SMART POWER?

Smart power is neither hard nor soft—it is the skillful combination of both. Smart power means developing an integrated strategy, resource base, and tool kit to achieve American objectives, drawing on both hard and soft power. It is an approach that underscores the necessity of a strong military, but also invests heavily in alliances, partnerships, and institutions at all levels to expand American influence and establish the legitimacy of American action. Providing for the global good is central to this effort because it helps America reconcile its overwhelming power with the rest of the world's interests and values.

Smart power means developing an integrated strategy, resource base, and tool kit to achieve American objectives, drawing on both hard and soft power.

Elements of this approach exist today in U.S. foreign policy, but they lack a cohesive rationale and institutional grounding. Three main obstacles exist.

First, U.S. foreign policy has tended to over-rely on hard power because it is the most direct and visible source of American strength. The Pentagon is the best trained and best resourced arm of the federal government. As a result, it tends to fill every void, even those that civilian instruments should fill. America must retain its military superiority, but in today's context, there are limits to what hard power can achieve on its own.

Second, U.S. foreign policy is still struggling to develop soft power instruments. Diplomatic tools and foreign assistance are often directed toward states, which increasingly compete for power with non-state actors within their borders. Diplomacy and foreign assistance are often underfunded and underused. These tools are neglected in

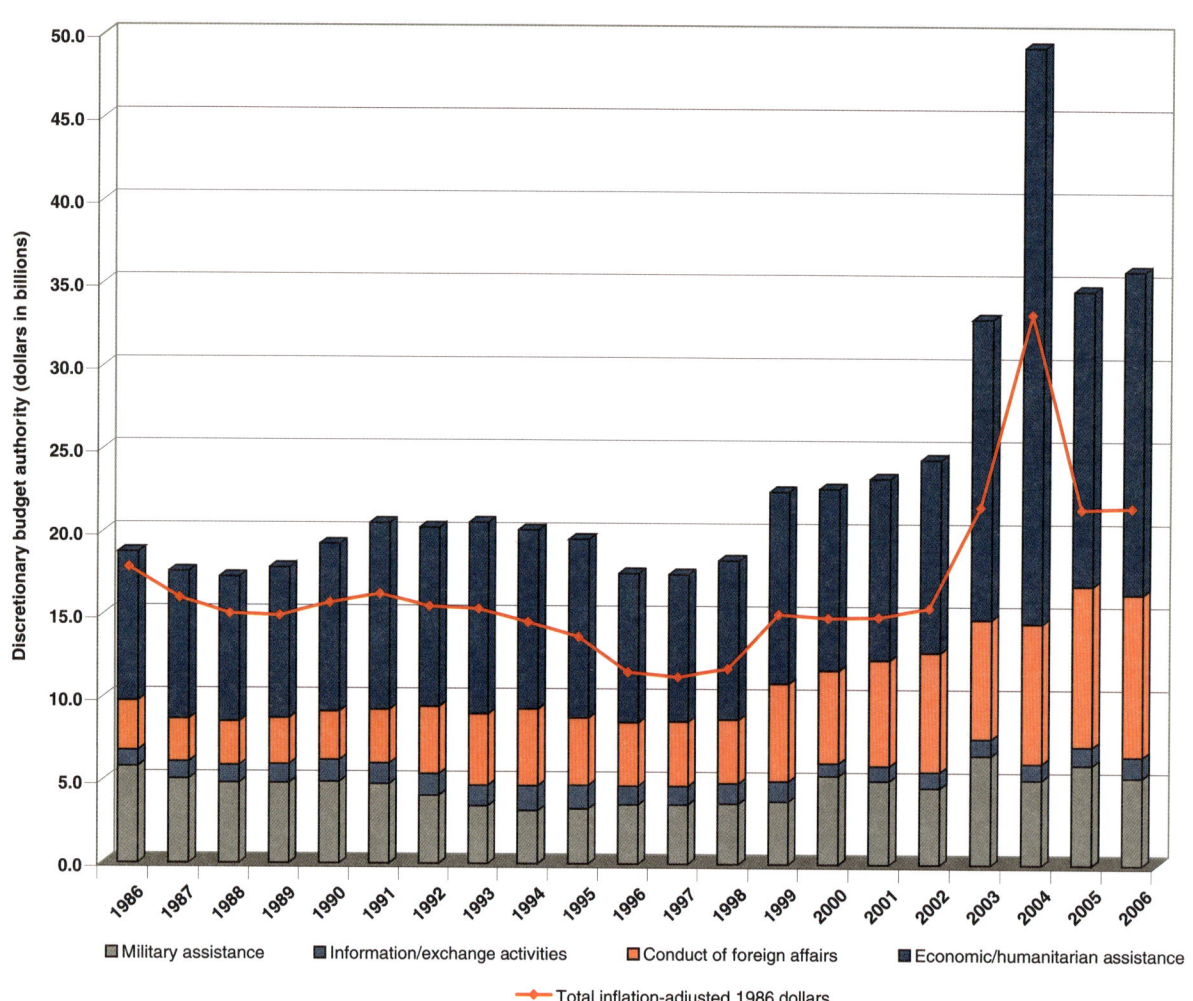

Figure 1. U.S. International Affairs Funding, 1986–2006*

*Budget function 150—international financial programs excluded.
Data source: U.S. Office of Management and Budget, public database.

> "The United States should be a beacon for the rest of the world—not out of step and out of favor."
>
> RICHARD L. ARMITAGE

part because of the difficulty of demonstrating their short-term impact on critical challenges. Figure 1 shows U.S. spending on international affairs over the past 20 years. Note that funding was generally stagnant for a decade. Increases in the early 1990s—due primarily to economic aid to Eastern and Central Europe—were offset by reductions in development assistance and public diplomacy funding. Increases from 1999 to 2002 were driven in part by security concerns following the embassy bombings in Nairobi and Dar el Salaam. Recent increases are on account of support to critical countries in the war on terror, the Millennium Challenge Corporation and PEPFAR initiatives, and humanitarian emergencies.

It should come as no surprise that some of the best-funded and most appreciated soft power tools have been humanitarian operations carried out by the U.S. military such as tsunami relief in Southeast Asia and the earthquake response in Pakistan, since these operations produced results that were clear, measurable, and unassailable. Wielding soft power is especially difficult, however, because many of America's soft power resources lie outside of government in the private sector and civil society, in its bilateral alliances, or through its participation in multilateral institutions.

Third, U.S. foreign policy institutions are fractured and compartmentalized. Coordination, where there is any, happens either at a relatively low level or else at the very highest levels of government—both typically in crisis settings that drive out long-range planning. Stovepiped institutional cultures inhibit joint action.

More thought should also be put into sequencing and integrating hard and soft power instruments, particularly in the same operating theater. Some elements of this approach are already occurring in the conduct of ongoing counterinsurgency, nation building, and counterterrorism operations—tasks that depend critically but only partially on hard power.

The United States has in its past wielded hard and soft power in concert, with each contributing a necessary component to a larger aim. We used hard power to deter the Soviet Union during the Cold War and soft power to rebuild Japan and Europe with the Marshall Plan and to establish institutions and norms that have become the core of the international system. Today's context presents a unique set of challenges, however, and requires a new way of thinking about American power.

TODAY'S CHALLENGES

The twenty-first century presents a number of unique foreign policy challenges for today's decisionmakers. These challenges exist at an international, transnational, and global level.

Despite America's status as the lone global power and concerns about the durability of the current international order, America should renew its commitment to the current order and help find a way for today's norms and institutions to accommodate rising powers that may hold a different set of principles and values. Furthermore, even countries invested in the current order may waver in their commitment to take action to minimize the threats posed by violent non-state actors and regional powers who challenge this order.

The information age has heightened political consciousness, but also made political groupings less cohesive. Small, adaptable, transnational networks have access to tools of destruction that are increasingly cheap, easy to conceal, and more readily available. Although the integration of the global economy has brought tremendous benefits, threats such as pandemic disease and the collapse of financial markets are more distributed and more likely to arise without warning.

The threat of widespread physical harm to the planet posed by nuclear catastrophe has existed for half a century, though the realization of the threat will become more likely as the number of nuclear weapons states increases. The potential security challenges posed by climate change raise the possibility of an entirely new set of threats for the United States to consider.

The next administration will need a strategy that speaks to each of these challenges. Whatever specific approach it decides to take, two principles will be certain:

First, an extra dollar spent on hard power will not necessarily bring an extra dollar's worth of security. It is difficult to know how to invest wisely when there is not a budget based on a strategy that specifies trade-offs among instruments. Moreover, hard power capabilities are a necessary but insufficient guarantee of security in today's context.

> An extra dollar spent on hard power will not necessarily bring an extra dollar's worth of security.

Second, success and failure will turn on the ability to win new allies and strengthen old ones both in government and civil society. The key is not how many enemies the United States kills, but how many allies it grows.

States and non-state actors who improve their ability to draw in allies will gain competitive advantages in today's environment. Those who alienate potential friends will stand at greater risk. China has invested in its soft power to ensure access to resources and to ensure against efforts to undermine its military modernization. Terrorists depend on their ability to attract support from the crowd at least as much as their ability to destroy the enemy's will to fight.

EXPORTING OPTIMISM, NOT FEAR

Since its founding, the United States has been willing to fight for universal ideals of liberty, equality, and justice. This higher purpose, sustained by military and economic might, attracted people and governments to our side through two world wars and five decades of the Cold War. Allies accepted that American interests may not always align entirely with their own, but U.S. leadership was still critical to realizing a more peaceful and prosperous world.

There have been times, however, when America's sense of purpose has fallen out of step with the world. Since 9/11, the United States has been exporting fear and anger rather than more tradi-

"Today's challenges require new types of institutions to extend American influence. We need a multilateral pluralism for the twenty-first century."

JOSEPH S. NYE, JR.

tional values of hope and optimism. Suspicions of American power have run deep. Even traditional allies have questioned whether America is hiding behind the righteousness of its ideals to pursue some other motive.

At the core of the problem is that America has made the war on terror the central component of its global engagement. This is not a partisan critique, nor a Pollyannaish appraisal of the threats facing America today. The threat from terrorists with global reach and ambition is real. It is likely to be with us for decades. Thwarting their hateful intentions is of fundamental importance and must be met with the sharp tip of America's sword. On this there can be no serious debate. But excessive use of force can actually abet terrorist recruitment among local populations. We must strike a balance between the use of force against irreconcilable extremists committed to violent struggle and other means of countering terrorism if we want to maintain our legitimacy.

What is apparent six years after September 11 is that a broader and more durable consensus is required to wage this struggle at home and abroad. The 2008 election cycle will inevitably bring forth partisan jockeying concerning which candidate and party will keep Americans most safe. This is a healthy and important debate, but one that should not preclude a bipartisan commitment to recognize and meet the global threat posed by terrorists and violent extremism. Such a commitment ought to be built upon the following four principles:

First, American leaders should stay on the offensive in countering terrorist aims abroad, but must also refuse to over-respond to their provocations. More attention ought to go toward preventing terrorists' access to weapons of mass destruction, but short of such a nightmare scenario, terrorists pose no existential threat to the United States. Their only hope—and indeed, their intended plan—is to use a sort of "jujitsu effect" in which they entice a large, powerful nation such as the United States to overreact and make choices that hurt itself. America must resist falling into traps that have grave strategic consequences beyond the costs of any isolated, small-scale attacks, regardless of the individual and collective pain they may cause.

Second, American leaders ought to eliminate the symbols that have come to represent the image of an intolerant, abusive, unjust America. The unfairness of such a characterization does not minimize its persuasive power abroad. Closing the Guantanamo Bay detention center is an obvious starting point and should lead to a broader rejection of torture and prisoner abuse. Guantanamo's very existence undermines America's ability to carry forth a message of principled optimism and hope. Although closing Guantanamo will be no simple matter, legal and practical constraints are surmountable if it should become a priority of American leadership, and planning for its closure should begin well before the next president takes office.

Third, we should use our diplomatic power for positive ends. Equally important to closing Guantanamo is expending political capital to end the corrosive effect of the Israeli-Palestinian conflict. The United States must resume its traditional role as an effective broker for peace in the Middle East, recognizing that all parties involved in the Israeli-Palestinian conflict have a responsibility to bring about a peaceful solution. Although we cannot want peace more than the parties themselves, we cannot be indifferent to the widespread suffering that this conflict perpetuates, nor the passionate feelings that it arouses on all sides. Many have rightly made this recommendation before, and many will do so in the future until a just peace can be realized. In the Middle East and elsewhere, effective American mediation confers global legitimacy and is a vital source of smart power.

Fourth, American leaders must provide the world with a positive vision greater than the war on terror. Americans need a shared aim to strive for, not simply a tactic to fight against. Efforts to pose counterterrorism operations as a global struggle between the forces of tyranny and the forces of freedom have not succeeded in drawing the world to our side. Freedom has always been part of the American narrative and should continue to be so, but too many in the Muslim world continue to read the war on terror as a war on Islam. Rather than unintentionally provoke a clash of civilizations, America's purpose should be to promote the elevation of civilizations and individuals.

In short, success in battling terrorism and restoring America's greatness depends on finding a new central premise for U.S. foreign policy to replace the war on terror. Taking its place should be an American commitment to providing for the global good. Such an approach derives from our principles, supports our interests, and strengthens our security.

MAINTAINING ALLIES, WINNING NEW PARTNERS

America is likely to remain the preponderant power in world politics after Iraq, but it will have to reengage other countries to share leadership. America's position as the lone global power is unlikely to last forever, and the United States must find ways of transforming its power into a moral consensus that ensures the willing acceptance if not active promotion of our values over time. This will require combining hard and soft power into a smart power strategy of working for the global good. America must learn to do things that others want and cannot do themselves, and to do so in a cooperative fashion.

Colonialism was an exploitative system that the United States has no intention of replicating. But America can learn a lesson from certain elements of Great Britain's strategy in the nineteenth century, when it was the world's foremost power. Great Britain took the lead in maintaining the balance of power in Europe, promoting an international economic system and maintaining freedom of

> In short, success in battling terrorism and restoring America's greatness depends on finding a new central premise for U.S. foreign policy to replace the War on Terror.

the seas. It benefited doubly from this—from the goods themselves and from the way they legitimized British power in the eyes of others. Policies based on broadly inclusive and far-sighted definitions of national interest are easier to make attractive to people overseas than policies that take a narrower perspective.

America has played a role in maintaining international order and providing for the global good since World War II. We took the lead in creating institutions such as the United Nations, World Bank, International Monetary Fund, and the General Agreement on Tariffs and Trade, all of which provided a framework of rules for maintaining international security and growing the world economy. This framework has been extended into new realms such as maritime security, financial markets, space exploration, cyberspace, drug trafficking, human trafficking, and terrorism.

The United States has provided a disproportionate share of the resources to address these challenges, but has also been the largest beneficiary. In the absence of U.S. leadership, regional powers would be unlikely to achieve the same degree of cooperation because of the difficulties of organizing collective action. Although it may be true that regional powers enjoy the benefits of this system without expending the same resources, American engagement is critical to any meaningful manifestation of global collective will.

Since the collapse of the Soviet Union, there has been a growing sense in some quarters of the United States, however, that providing for the global good has become less necessary or even peripheral to the real problems of the day. Particularly after 9/11, international norms and institutions appeared to some to constrain American behavior in ways that made Americans less safe. This belief has contributed to the growing reliance on U.S. hard power.

When the United States chooses to go it alone, however, it raises doubts about the legitimacy of American actions and creates widespread anxieties about how we will use our overwhelming power abroad. Multilateral consultation remains a more effective means of generating soft power and legitimacy than unilateral assertions of values. A general presumption in favor of multilateralism need not be a straightjacket, though. Working with others must always benefit the United States as well.

On the flip side, multilateralism cannot be merely a public relations strategy designed to provide political cover for unilateral action. No country likes to feel manipulated, even by soft power. America's international reputation is more of a byproduct than an outcome that can be brought about through concerted effort. Striving for admiration on the world stage for its own sake is ignoble and bound to fail. The United States must genuinely institutionalize the value of winning allies to its side in order to achieve its objectives abroad.

STARTING AT HOME

As part of this commission's work, we sent a commissioner and staff around the United States to engage in a listening tour with the American people. We called this effort our "Dialogue with America." What we heard diverged from the conventional wisdom in Washington of an inward-looking electorate. Instead we heard a universal desire on the part of Americans to improve their country's image in the world and tap into its vast potential for good. Americans from across the political spectrum believed, however, that we first needed to "get America right" before we can be credible to the world.

The United States cannot ask the world to admire us if we do not behave admirably. We cannot ask the world to follow our lead if we prove ourselves ineffective. One of the terrible lasting impressions of Hurricane Katrina is that the U.S. government is both unfair and inept in the face of real challenges that impact people's lives. We have sent the same message internationally with our immigration policy.

Becoming a smarter power requires more than changes in policy, though; it requires a greater investment in human capital at home. America's education system is one of our greatest soft power assets, and yet there are signs of lagging American competitiveness in vital areas of science and technology. We need to ensure that we are producing workers and citizens who can understand and compete in an increasingly globalized world.

America is a great nation. There is no reason why the United States cannot regain its standing and influence in the world at the same time as it builds up its hard power for the twenty-first century. The five recommendations found within this report are meant to signal the types of initiatives the next administration could take to reinvigorate America's soft power. The report begins with a diagnosis of America's waning influence and concludes by looking at some of the institutional and budgetary implications of a smart power strategy.

A smarter, more secure America is one that can rediscover its greatness as a source of inspiring ideas and practical solutions for people in all corners of the world.

COMMISSION REPORT

PART I | DIAGNOSIS | WANING INFLUENCE

People and governments abroad are at some level dissatisfied with American leadership. Allies and adversaries alike openly criticize U.S. policy. One opinion poll after another has demonstrated that America's reputation, standing, and influence are at all-time lows, and possibly sinking further. Take just five recent examples:

- A WorldPublicOpinion Poll in June 2007 found that majorities in 10 of 15 countries polled did not trust the United States to act responsibly.

- A BBC World Service poll of more than 26,000 people across 25 different countries in January 2007 revealed that one in two says the United States is playing a mainly negative role in the world.

- A poll commissioned by newspapers in Canada, Britain, and Mexico surveyed 3,000 people in late 2006 and found that a majority in all three countries view President Bush as a threat to world peace comparable to Iran's Mahmoud Ahmadinejad, North Korea's Kim Jong Il, and Hezbollah's Hassan Nasrallah.

- A Zogby poll of five Middle East countries (Saudi Arabia, Egypt, Morocco, Jordan, and Lebanon) from late 2006 found that a majority in all five reported that their opinion of the United States had gotten worse in the past year.

- The Pew Global Attitudes Project revealed in 2006 that there has been a substantial decline in the opinion of foreigners toward the American people since 2002, particularly in Europe.

This onslaught of negative reporting on how the world views America prompts three immediate questions:

1. Is it that bad? Are negative views of America as prevalent and intense in all regions of the world?

2. Does it matter? Do negative views reflect a diminished American ability to achieve its national interests and uphold its values?

3. Can it be fixed? If American influence has waned, what are the main causes of its decline, and what are the main opportunities to reverse course?

America's reputation, standing, and influence in the world matter for the security and prosperity of the United States. There is little question that America's diminished standing abroad has

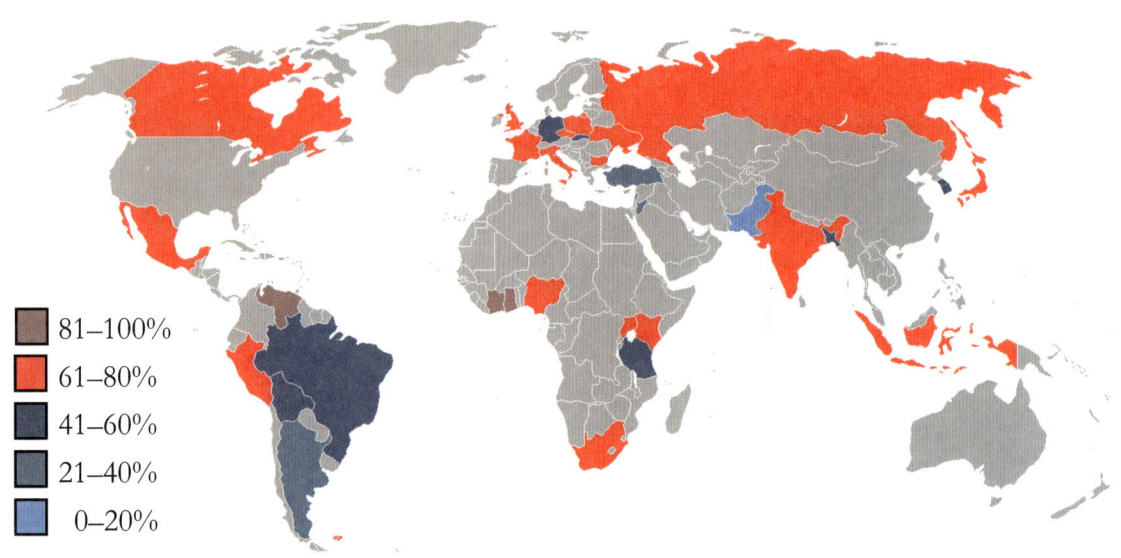

Favorable Opinion of United States 2002

Data source: Pew Research Center, The Pew Global Attitudes Survey, "What the World Thinks in 2002," December 2002.

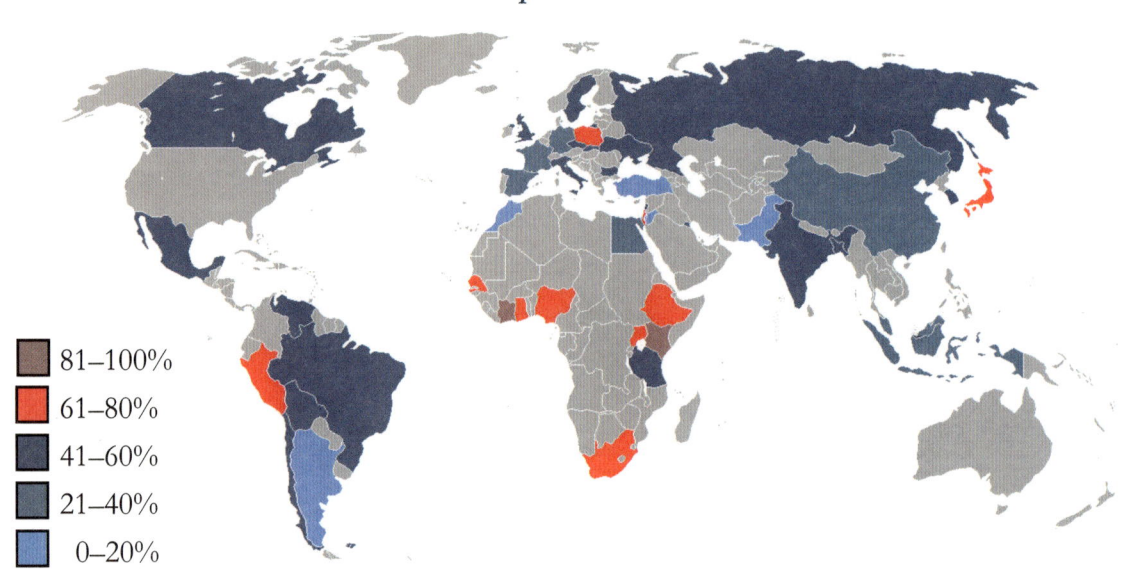

Favorable Opinion of United States 2007

Data source: Pew Research Center, The Pew Global Attitudes Survey, "Global Unease with Major World Powers: 47-Nation Pew Global Attitudes Survey," June 2007.

meant that the United States has had increased difficulty in accomplishing its goals. For foreign leaders, standing alongside U.S. policy has often appeared to be the "kiss of death." The Turkish parliament's decision to refuse to allow American troops to use its territory as a staging ground for the invasion of Iraq in 2003 had grave consequences for U.S. policy.

America may be less well regarded today than at any time in its history, but it is not too late to reverse this trend, even in the Arab and Muslim world. Doing so, however, will require a strategy that strikes a new balance between the use of hard and soft power and that integrates these elements into a smarter approach to the main challenges facing the United States and the global community.

CAUSES OF DECLINE

How did the United States lose the stature and goodwill it had accumulated during the Cold War and in its immediate aftermath? Surely the war in Iraq—hugely unpopular during the run-up to war five years back and even more so today—is a major factor. But this is too convenient and superficial an explanation. America's deteriorating esteem started well before the war in Iraq and will not be resolved simply by ending that conflict. There are at least five significant causes of America's declining influence:

- America's sole superpower status. Paradoxically, the fall of the Soviet Union hastened America's declining stature. When the Cold War ended, America stood alone as the towering superpower on the world stage, while Cold War allies, less dependent on U.S. assistance or security guarantees, started to resent America's unbounded dominance. This came at a time when America's economy was booming and America seemed unstoppable. World leaders decried American "hyperpower" and spoke openly of creating a multipolar world to counterbalance the United States. The subsequent collapse of Enron and the burst of the "dot-com" financial bubble led to a widely held sentiment that America's power base was flawed and even illegitimate.

- Reaction against globalization. Revolutionary technological advances in communications (such as global, instantaneous telephone and Internet service), transportation (such as the containerization of cargo shipments and the growth of air transportation), and financial services transformed the world economy during the past two decades. Suddenly the rules changed, opening great opportunities in virtually every country. But globalization also introduced forces into societies that threatened existing norms and set off difficult and painful domestic adjustments. Many abroad view the United States as the main promoter and beneficiary of globalization and blame

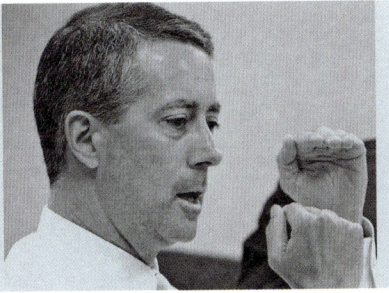

"Intelligence—meaning a deep understanding—is more important and in many ways more difficult to achieve than ever before."

MAC THORNBERRY

PART I: DIAGNOSIS 19

America for jobs lost and what they perceive as an assault on their traditions and culture.

- **America's isolation from agreements and institutions with widespread international support.** The United States has rejected a number of recent international initiatives that were popular abroad but lacked concerted support inside the United States. These included the Kyoto Protocol on climate change, the International Criminal Court, the Mine Ban Treaty, and the Convention on the Rights of the Child. Because the United States did not always offer superior alternatives to these initiatives, many abroad began to view America as rejectionist, opposing progress on matters that enjoyed broad international appeal. Similarly, as the credibility and authority of the United Nations have grown in many nations around the world, a significant part of the United States—rightly or wrongly—continues to view the United Nations as an institution in decline. Many nations have begun to look to the United Nations as a venue to constrain America's unbounded power since the Cold War, adding to America's estrangement.

- **America's response to 9/11.** Americans were shocked that terrorists, hiding among us for months, plotted the surprise attack on 9/11. Once a proud and confident nation, suddenly America became angry and frightened. We restricted access to visas and surrounded our embassies with concrete barriers and barbed wire. We demanded foreign countries accept American customs inspectors at their shipping ports, implying that foreigners could not be trusted. We embraced a simplistic "you are either with us or against us" approach and applied it to complex situations that demanded a more sophisticated policy response. And we adopted a new set of procedures in the "global war on terrorism"—secret prisons in foreign countries, secret "rendition" of suspects, detention of "unlawful enemy combatants" without judicial review, warrantless and unsupervised electronic surveillance procedures, and "enhanced interrogation procedures" that the world believes constitutes torture. In short, we applied methods that we had previously decried when used by other governments, fueling a widespread belief that we hold a double standard.

- **Perceptions of American incompetence.** Throughout the Cold War, America projected an image of vast technical competence. We sent human beings to the moon. We coordinated the eradication of small pox. We conducted winning wars in Iraq in 1991 and Kosovo in 1999 that demonstrated a towering technical proficiency. We gave the world the impression that we could master almost any technical problem. But recently we have projected a different image. Our weak response to the catastrophe caused by Hurricane Katrina and our inability to restore civil order and basic services such as electricity, water, and sanitation to Iraq have created the impression that America may have lost some of its technical edge.

Taken together, these factors have produced a startling erosion of standing in the world. To be sure, as CSIS scholars identified in the regional surveys that follow, America still enjoys a strong reputation in many parts of the world. People may not like America's current policies or leaders, but there is still a strong attraction to the idea of

America. The United States is still seen as a land of opportunity and as the nation that must lead if there are to be solutions to global problems.

REGIONAL ASSESSMENTS

CSIS regional scholars assessed how various countries and regions view the United States and the corresponding effect on U.S. influence. The result is a more complex picture than suggested by poll numbers or by the notion that electing a new president and withdrawing troops from Iraq will automatically restore America's standing in the world.

Europe

The transatlantic relationship has long been one of the strongest partnerships in the international system. The United States cannot address global challenges without Europe's active involvement, but many Europeans today have a diminished confidence in the alliance.

The roots of this separation lie in divergent threat assessments from the 1990s and differing lessons from the Kosovo intervention. The relationship was further strained in the early days of the Bush administration with the decision to withdraw from the Anti-Ballistic Missile treaty, rejection of the Kyoto Protocol, and failure to join the International Criminal Court.

The run-up to and waging of the war in Iraq, including the Abu Ghraib abuses, have made this divide most apparent, as has U.S. conduct in the war on terrorism (Guantanamo Bay and extraordinary rendition, for example). Europe perceives that America lacks a commitment to the types of legal, institutional, and multilateral frameworks that Europe has built in the European Union.

Within Europe, countries continue to look inward at European integration, punctuated by a more secure and assertive Germany and France and a younger generation of Europeans with less knowledge of and interest in the United States. Above all, Europeans do not want to be simply informed about American decisions; they want to be consulted and treated as partners.

Nonetheless, cooperation continues below the surface on a host of key issues, and more positive views of the United States can be found in Central and Eastern Europe—partly on account of the historic wariness those countries feel toward a strengthening Russia and Germany.

Russia

U.S.-Russian relations are chillier than they have been at any time since the end of the Cold War. Awash in petrodollars, Russia's effort to reassert its interests has led to increased friction with Europe and the United States.

Most Russians today read American initiatives and aid as part of a hidden agenda to undermine Russia's recovery. Historically, negative feelings about the United States resurfaced in the late 1990s with the collapse of the ruble and NATO's use of force in Kosovo.

Russian president Vladimir Putin's Munich speech earlier this year was indicative of broader feelings within Russia that efforts to expand NATO,

develop a Ballistic Missile Defense program, and spread democracy via the "colored revolutions" are part of a broader U.S. containment policy aimed against Russia. Even the failure of the United States to repeal the 1974 Jackson-Vanik amendment is interpreted as an effort to hold back the Russian economy.

Putin has capitalized on these feelings to spur nationalist sentiment and expand his authoritarian rule, isolating traditional allies of America who in turn feel abandoned by the United States.

Americas

Although Canada and Mexico are the first and third largest trading partners of the United States and our most important sources of imported oil, the feeling persists—particularly in Central and South America—that the United States has neglected its neighbors to the south.

With the end of the Cold War, the United States scaled back much of its engagement and programming, including its public diplomacy efforts. The wave of optimism that existed in the early 1990s as regional governments transitioned from military dictatorships to democratic civilian regimes was stifled by serious financial crises and the failure of most governments to take the next generation of political and economic reforms.

More recently, a strong and growing sentiment—promoted by a new generation of populist leaders—has also emerged in the region that U.S.-led globalization has left large pockets of Latin American societies behind. These trends, together with fears of U.S. unilateralism and disregard for international law and institutions, are tapping into old threads of anti-Americanism.

U.S. policy toward Cuba is also a major sticking point in the region. And yet, while the war in Iraq is widely unpopular, many remain open to U.S. leadership.

Africa

Unlike most regions of the world, Africans by and large view the United States as a positive force in the world.

America's renewed commitment to Africa relates to the continent's rising strategic stakes as an important source of energy supplies, a possible safe haven for terrorist groups, a transit node of illegal trafficking in drugs, arms, and people, and a growing voice in multilateral institutions. U.S. domestic constituencies have made HIV/AIDS and Darfur two signature moral issues of our time.

The current U.S. administration has launched an array of soft power initiatives in Africa that reflect a real commitment to alter the status quo, including the $15 billion President's Emergency Program for AIDS relief (PEPFAR), much of which is dedicated to Africa; the Millennium Challenge Account that provides development aid to well-governed, free-market countries; a major initiative on malaria; and an overall tripling of U.S. development assistance levels.

U.S. military efforts to build partnerships with, and the capabilities of, African armed forces

have also increased, including through the African Contingency Operations Training Assistance (ACOTA) program and the newly established Africa Command. The intervention of U.S. troops in Liberia in 2003 to ensure the departure of Charles Taylor—although limited in scope—was a major shift away from the apprehension generated by the failed Somalia mission in 1993.

Nonetheless, resentment remains on the continent over the perceived hypocrisy of the global trade regime, and competition has heightened with Chinese investment and assistance that is free of political conditionality.

Middle East
There is no region of the world in which U.S. standing has fallen further or more precipitously than in the Middle East.

A decade ago, the United States was generally seen as a guarantor of security, an effective mediator, and an intellectual colossus. The collapse of the Arab-Israeli peace process, the Iraq War, the perceived conflict with Islam, a resurgent Iran, exploding wealth in Gulf nations, and more politically aware populations mean that the United States is now at a distinct disadvantage in the region.

America is still relevant, but it has been weakened. Neither a new message nor a single regional conference to address Iraq, the Arab-Israeli conflict, or Iran will be enough to turn this tide.

One of the striking developments of the last several years has been the way in which the number of countries in the Middle East that are outright foes of the United States has been reduced to two—Iran and Syria. And yet, traditional American partners have moved swiftly to establish greater distance from the United States.

Perhaps the most profound problem the United States faces in the Middle East is the deep and growing hostility toward America among what should be the moderate middle of these societies. It is among this group that the hopes and aspirations of hundreds of millions of people are turning away from a close relationship with the United States.

South Asia
South Asia is dominated by the fate of two countries on different trajectories and with different views of the United States.

Today, India generally has an optimistic view of its own future. There is a strong sense that an expanding relationship with the United States is helping to launch India onto the world stage, despite the Indian government's apparent inability to bring the Indo-U.S. nuclear deal to completion for the time being and despite misgivings about the implications of U.S. policy in Iraq.

One of the strongest assets of the U.S. relationship with India is the expanding connection between Indian and American people. The United States, having been for some decades a symbol of India's subordinate status in the world, is now to a significant extent seen as a vehicle for its emergence as a global power.

In contrast, Pakistanis see their relationship with the United States as a history of intense collaborations followed by American betrayals, the next of which may be lurking around the corner in a deteriorating Afghanistan. The potential for crises emerging either within Pakistan or between Pakistan and the United States are high given the intense domestic political challenges facing Islamabad and the antiterrorism effort ongoing on the Afghanistan border.

America's close ties with Pakistan's leaders are both a major asset and a major liability in a domestic political context. Despite significant and timely U.S. earthquake relief in 2005, U.S. policy is seen as anti-Muslim, in effect if not in intention, even as Pakistanis try to use their relationship with the United States to solve their internal problems.

Southeast Asia
The United States still enjoys an advantageous position in Southeast Asia due to its status as a guarantor of regional stability and source of economic assets.

Although Southeast Asian governments continue to rely on the U.S. security guarantee offered through bilateral alliances and U.S. military presence to maintain a regional balance of power, the failure of the United States to come to the region's aid in its time of need during the 1997–1998 Asian financial crisis left a lasting impression of uncertainty about the U.S. commitment when the region's interests are at stake.

The ensuing IMF austerity packages, the Iraq War, the early U.S. focus on the region as a "second front" in a global war on terrorism, and perceived American disregard for "the ASEAN way" of dialogue, multilateral consultation, and modesty have only exacerbated the region's concern. The quick and effective U.S. response to the 2004 tsunami improved views of the United States only temporarily.

At the same time, the Association of Southeast Asian Nations (ASEAN) has become the centerpiece for nascent development of a distinct pan-Asian regional identity to deal with regional problems. U.S. absence from emerging institutions threatens to affect U.S. credibility and relevance in the region, at times to the benefit of China. Overall, however, Southeast Asia wants to avoid having to choose between Washington and Beijing.

Northeast Asia
Although polling data suggest that positive public opinion toward the United States in Northeast Asia has declined over the past few years, the downturn has not been as precipitous as in other regions in the world.

The U.S.-Japan alliance is the indispensable core of America's footprint in Asia and the foundation for peace and stability in the region. The relationship has evolved over time, but remains one of America's most important strategic partnerships. That nearly two-thirds of Japanese people hold a favorable opinion of the United States reflects the fact that, on balance, Japan too appreciates the benefits of the alliance.

In contrast, a majority of South Koreans see U.S. influence as negative. They continue to see value in the alliance with the United States, but are frustrated with their enduring dependence on Washington for security and perceived U.S. insensitivity to their interests, particularly on North Korea. Seoul wants a more mature and equitable partnership with Washington in advancing mutual regional and global interests.

Perhaps no single bilateral relationship will affect global security and prosperity more than ties between the United States and China. Most Chinese maintain a generally positive view of American people, culture, and values, but there is also a long-standing perception that America seeks to interfere in internal Chinese affairs and contain Chinese influence abroad. Past incidents between the United States and China, such as the accidental bombing of the Chinese embassy in Belgrade in 1999 and the 2001 spy plane standoff, continue to irritate Chinese sentiment, underscoring the notion among Chinese that the United States seeks to undermine China's rise.

CHINESE SOFT POWER

Will Beijing soon become a viable alternative to American leadership? This is a much-debated question within policy circles in the United States, and many American experts fear a zero-sum game with China as the victor.

With Washington preoccupied in the Middle East, China has deftly stepped into the vacuum left by the United States, primarily to pursue its own economic interests, but possibly also to pursue its long-term strategic goals of becoming a global power rather than simply a regional one. China has taken a two-pronged approach, strengthening its hard power resources while simultaneously expanding its soft power influence.

The most visible example of China's growing soft power is Beijing's embrace of, and at times leadership in, multilateral organizations where the U.S. role has diminished or is absent altogether, particularly in China's own backyard. Underscoring its commitment to a "good neighbor" policy, China has resolved numerous territorial disputes in the region. Beijing has also signaled its respect for "the ASEAN Way," which is mostly dismissed by the United States, by becoming actively involved in Asian security and political arrangements, such as the ASEAN Regional Forum (ARF), the ASEAN + 3 process, the Shanghai Cooperation Organization (SCO), and the East Asia Summit. Beijing has placed strong emphasis on common economic development, including pursuit of a free trade agreement with ASEAN and, further north, with the Republic of Korea.

From Latin America to Africa to the Middle East, Beijing is selling into new markets, devouring natural resources, making lucrative oil deals,

"America's continued success in today's globalized world is contingent on our ability to engage, not demonize, dynamic powers like China."

MAURICE R. GREENBERG

forgiving debt, and generally offering aid and friendship free of political conditionality—thus building global goodwill and political influence despite signs of resentment in some quarters. For example, the "Beijing alternative" provides African nations with an option that places fewer conditions on aid and asks fewer questions about internal affairs than does Washington. Many in Latin America are also increasingly moving toward a "Pacific view" that looks to China to fill the perceived gap left by U.S. disinterest.

Even in Western democracies, many countries view China as playing an increasingly constructive role in global affairs despite its close relations with rogue and authoritarian states such as Sudan, Burma, and Iran. Many cite Beijing's growing engagement in UN peacekeeping missions and its role in the Six Party Talks on North Korea as evidence of its efforts toward becoming a truly responsible stakeholder within the global community. There may still be a healthy dose of skepticism about China and its future intentions and goals, but nonetheless, in general, China has risen in global public opinion in recent years.

China's soft power is likely to continue to grow, but this does not necessarily mean that Washington and Beijing are on a collision course, fighting for global influence. First, a number of factors ultimately will limit China's soft power, including its own domestic political, socioeconomic, and environmental challenges. Second, there are a number of critical areas of mutual interest between the United States and China on which the two powers can work together—and in some cases already are. Energy security and environmental stewardship top that list, along with other transnational issues such as public health and nonproliferation.

Finally, global leadership does not have to be a zero-sum game. China can only become preeminent if the United States continues to allow its own powers of attraction to atrophy.

PART II | A SMART POWER STRATEGY

This section provides recommendations to the next president of the United States on potential ingredients of a smart power strategy. It is not designed to be a comprehensive national security strategy, but a set of policies that could help the United States become smarter and more secure through investments in the global good.

1 ALLIANCES, PARTNERSHIPS, AND INSTITUTIONS

REBUILDING THE FOUNDATION TO ADDRESS GLOBAL CHALLENGES

The United States generally has three options when responding to global challenges. First, it can proceed unilaterally. This approach provides freedom of action but risks international opposition and isolation. Unilateral action also misses out on the financial and operational benefits of allied support. American political leaders have debated the efficacy of unilateralism in recent years. Although no president will cede the option of unilateral action, the United States understands full well the perils of this approach and the benefits of allies and partners.

Second, the United States can assemble ad hoc coalitions, employing consensus-based internationalism. This approach still enjoys the benefits of burden sharing, but U.S.-led coalitions are free from the constraints imposed by alliance partners who may have divergent assessments or goals. Although consensus-based internationalism enables the United States to address the challenges at hand, it also requires considerable effort to build a cohort of likeminded states. The success of such efforts depends to large extent on preexisting alliance structures. Consensus-based internationalism does little to build a foundation to address future challenges. The next president should view consensus-based internationalism as a pragmatic, short-term option that has limited value beyond the coalition's immediate objectives.

Third, the United States can work through treaties, alliances, and multilateral organizations—so-called norms-based internationalism. Formal agreements and global norms provide the United States with the standing capacity to act in conjunction with allies at the times we need them most. This approach served the United States well in the Cold War and should be the bedrock of our internationalism going forward.

Figure 2. U.S. International Affairs Multilateral Funding, 1986–2006

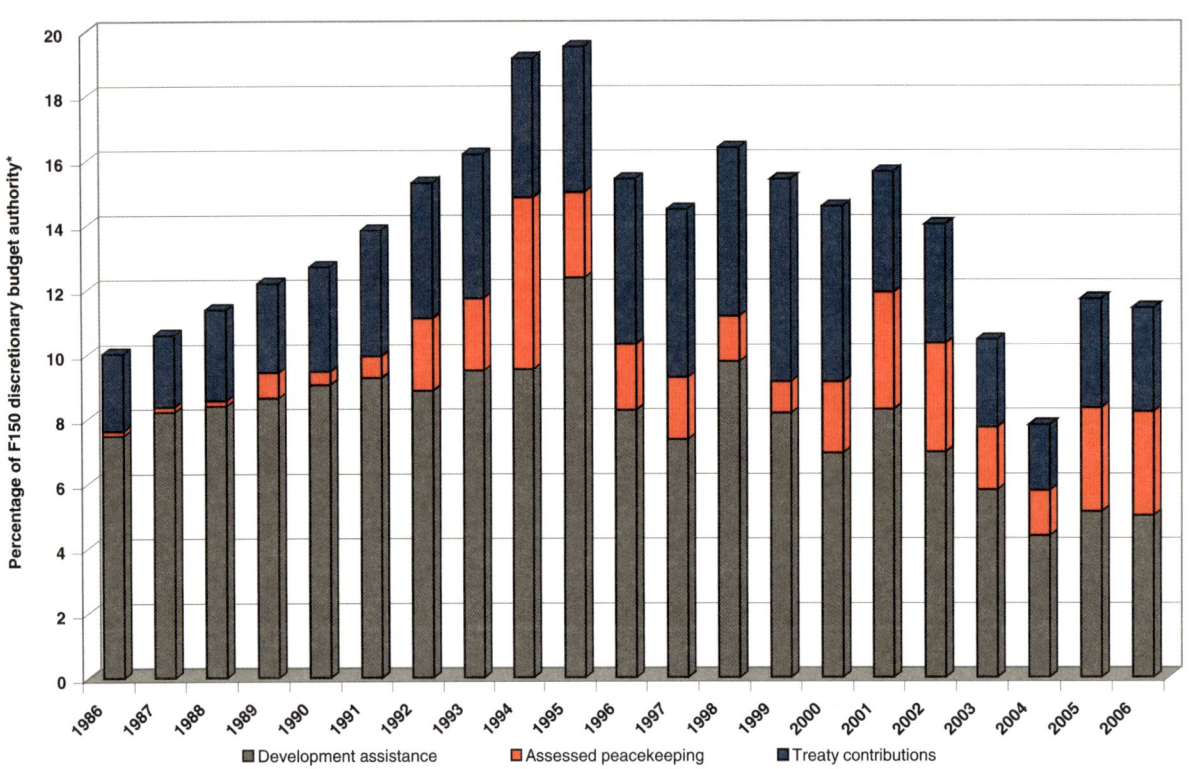

*Total excludes international financial programs.

Data source: U.S. Office of Management and Budget, public database.

Throughout the Cold War, American leaders defined internationalism in terms of treaties and institutions. The United States invested heavily in the United Nations, World Bank, and International Monetary Fund, signed binding treaties with other countries to station U.S. forces abroad as the bedrock of our alliances, and helped to develop a growing body of international law with a particular focus on individual political rights. Alongside America's nuclear deterrent, this strategy contributed to U.S. success in containing Soviet expansion.

Although the United States never relied entirely on treaties and institutions during this period, American leaders tended to view them as extensions of U.S. influence. They were tools that helped the United States to engage and counter the Soviets on multiple levels and in multiple theaters, diminishing the risk of overreliance on any single facet of American power.

In recent years, however, an increasing number of American leaders have turned away from a norms-based approach to global engagement.

> "Multilateral capacity building goes beyond the instant coffee of coalition building."
>
> THOMAS R. PICKERING

They have come to view international law as suggestive rather than binding, alliances as outdated and dispensable, and international institutions as decrepit or hostile. Some U.S. leaders have preferred to rely on coalitions of the willing to achieve American objectives rather than on formal alliance structures or multilateral approaches that depend upon UN sanction. Figure 2 shows U.S. multilateral funding over the past 20 years, excluding international financial programs. Note the decrease following immediate post–Cold War peaks. Recent increases are due to the growing demands of UN peacekeeping operations.

Although norms-based internationalism requires institutions and agreements that are updated and capable of addressing today's challenges—particularly the rise of non-state actors—investing in such a system provides both short-term and long-term benefits beyond what unilateral action or consensus-based internationalism can bring.

In the short term, global norms and institutions allow the United States to address many hazards concurrently without having to build a consensus in response to every new challenge. Because of America's global interests and responsibilities, it often finds itself managing numerous crises simultaneously. Some of these challenges may be regional in nature and require regional institutions to address. Others may be transnational and require a multitude of state actors in concerted action over time—something only norms-based internationalism can yield.

In the long run, investing in institutions and global norms works to preserve U.S. ideas, values, and interests into the future. This is particularly important if the relative weight of non-Western powers was to increase in the years ahead and America was to become less able to assert itself internationally.

The next U.S. administration will come to power with its own ideas about which aspects of the current international architecture are worth preserving. What is needed today is a clear-headed analysis of which aspects of the international system work to extend American power in pursuit of the global good, which work to dilute it, and which simply do not work. The next president should strike a new consensus at home and abroad for finding normative solutions to pragmatic challenges.

Regardless of who sits in the White House, however, America must again play a role in shaping the global agenda and international system. Leading will require the confidence and patience to work effectively in multilateral settings where new players seek to rally countries against us.

Three approaches could help to extend American influence as a force for good—renewing our commitment to the United Nations, reinvigorating our alliances, and working to erase the perception that the United States has double standards when it comes to abiding by international law.

Today it is uncertain whether the institution can still play a determining role in the main peace and security challenges of the twenty-first cen-

"Investing in UN peacekeeping is cost-effective and makes sense for American interests."

GEORGE RUPP

UNITED NATIONS

The United Nations means different things to different people—to some it is mankind's last best hope for a peaceful and prosperous world. For others, it is a venal, ineffective institution that subjects America's goals to the vile intentions of rights-abusing regimes. Both of these descriptions are of course caricatures, but herein lies the paradox of the United Nations—it is the main source of legitimacy in international affairs for much of the world, and yet a number of its internal transgressions (the 2004 Oil for Food scandal) and structural deficiencies (the lack of broader representation on the Security Council) call that very legitimacy into question.

Allied powers created the United Nations after World War II to avoid the horrible wars that devastated the early part of the twentieth century.

tury. The credibility of the Security Council is at an all-time low, and the U.S.-UN relationship has been strained nearly to the breaking point.

America needs the United Nations, but we need a better one than we have at present. The organization needs much stronger and accountable management, such as what was outlined in the 2005 Gingrich-Mitchell Task Force on UN Reform. The true strength of the United Nations still lies in the norms embedded in its charter—values that greatly benefit the United States if pursued objectively—as well as in its operational departments and agencies that can help the United States to implement a smart power strategy.

In particular, the United Nations could play an active role in furthering America's desire to promote the global good in four key areas: peacekeeping and peacebuilding; counterterrorism; global health; and energy and climate.

Peacekeeping and Peacebuilding. The best chance of sustaining the legitimacy and effectiveness for international peacekeeping and peacebuilding interventions over time derives from a solid U.S.-UN partnership. Right now the United Nations has more than 100,000 peacekeepers deployed around the world, making it the second-largest international security provider behind the United States. It is also playing a leading role in building the capacity of the African Union to address the disaster in Darfur. The next administration should support the work of UN institutions that further U.S. goals in a cost-effective manner, such as the UN Department of Peacekeeping Operations (UNDPKO) and the new Peacebuilding Commission and Support Office. Figure 3 shows U.S. multilateral funding in 2006. U.S. financial support for UN peacekeeping operations hit a 20-year high of nearly $1.2 billion in 2006, up from $28 million in 1986.

Counterterrorism. The United Nations will never replace the role states play in meeting the threat of terrorism, but it can help to coordinate thinking and action on addressing the conditions conducive to the threat of terrorism and on breaking the chain of radicalization. Avoiding a "made in America" stamp in some instances may help the United States to pursue a more successful counterterrorism approach.

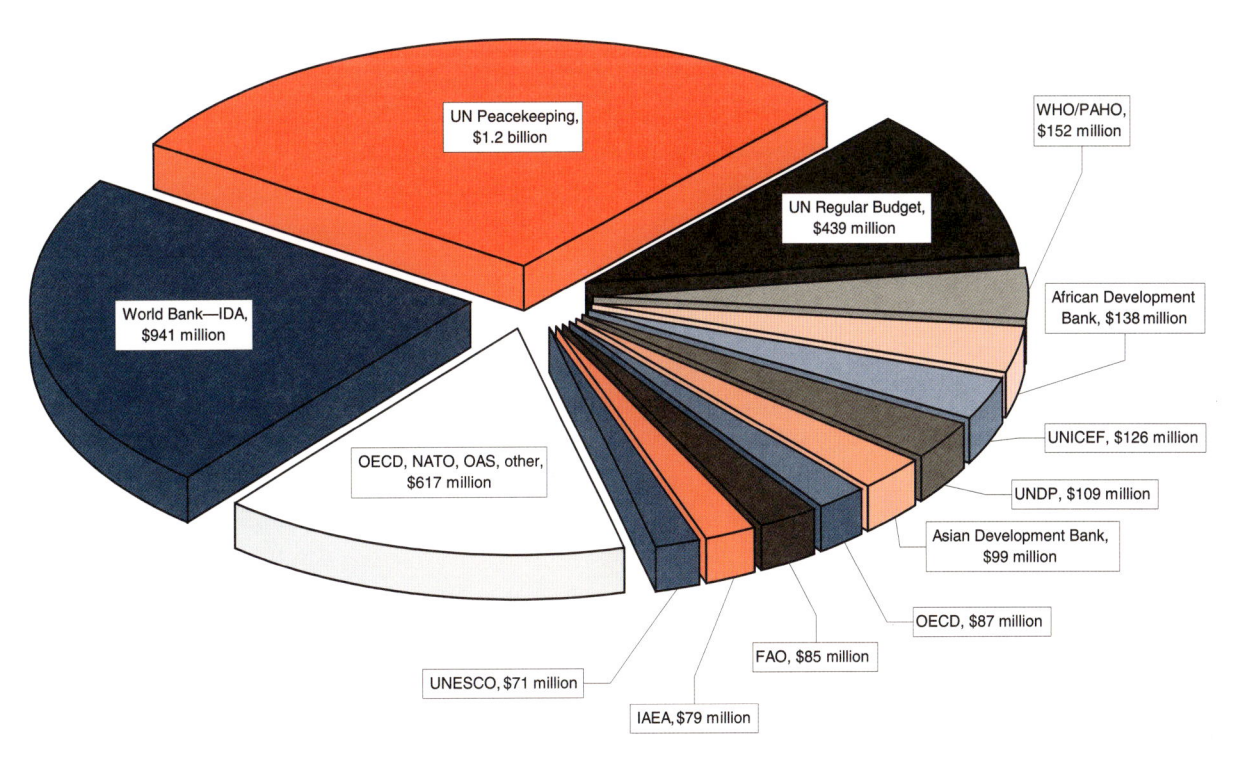

Figure 3. U.S. International Affairs Multilateral Funding, 2006*

- UN Peacekeeping, $1.2 billion
- World Bank—IDA, $941 million
- OECD, NATO, OAS, other, $617 million
- UN Regular Budget, $439 million
- WHO/PAHO, $152 million
- African Development Bank, $138 million
- UNICEF, $126 million
- UNDP, $109 million
- Asian Development Bank, $99 million
- OECD, $87 million
- FAO, $85 million
- IAEA, $79 million
- UNESCO, $71 million

*Budget function 150—international affairs only. Excludes amounts appropriated to other agencies (e.g., DHHS, DOL).

Data sources: U.S. Office of Management and Budget, public database; U.S. Department of State, Congressional Budget Justifications, FY 2008.

Note: IDA = International Development Association; OECD = Organization for Economic Cooperation and Development; OAS = Organization for American States; WHO/PAHO = World Health Organization/Pan American Health Organization; UNDP = United Nations Development Program; FAO = Food and Agriculture Organization; IAEA = International Atomic Energy Agency.

Global Health. The increase in funds devoted to global public health in recent years from both the public and private sectors does little to help build the coherence necessary for a successful international response. The United Nations can play a role here, mainly through the World Health Organization, in developing common systems and approaches. The next chapter on global development addresses this issue in greater depth.

Energy and Climate. The challenges of energy insecurity and climate change are precisely the sort of global threats that the United Nations could help to address. In recent years, the United Nations has played a marginal role in policy coordination for energy and climate beyond helping to forge a scientific consensus on global warming and mobilize global will. The December 2007 UN Climate Change Conference in Bali may create new demands for coordination and expertise in helping to implement international agreements. Chapter 5 on technology and innovation addresses energy insecurity and climate change more fully.

America's souring on the United Nations and failing to pay its dues to the UN have hurt our country internationally. The next administration should weigh the most effective ways of leveraging the UN to become a better international partner.

ALLIANCES

The U.S. alliance system negotiated during the last half century consists of nearly 100 formal treaty arrangements and security commitments. Alliances extend American power by increasing legitimacy and burden sharing, by facilitating consultation and interoperability, and by helping to address unforeseen challenges without the start-up costs of coalition building. Alliances also preserve American power by diminishing the chances of bandwagoning or balancing against the United States.

Rather than view these agreements as hindrances to American action, the next president ought to view this alliance network as a force multiplier. We have preferred coalitions of the willing lately, but these are impossible to sustain without the investments made in our formal alliances in Europe and East Asia. The cooperation of America's allies will be vital to our ability to tackle twenty-first century problems.

A number of opportunities to bolster American alliances exist today. What is required on the most basic level is simply the willingness of the next president to signal an enduring commitment to our European and East Asian allies. For example, the North Atlantic Treaty Organization (NATO) stands at a crossroads, unsure of its broader strategic purpose following the Soviet collapse. Differing views exist in both the United States and Europe as to whether now is the proper time to rethink NATO's strategic rationale. Until such time as a consensus emerges, the United States should concentrate on ensuring that NATO's efforts in Afghanistan are successful by maintaining European support and enhancing the alliance's peacekeeping and state-building capabilities.

In Asia, the United States has traditionally sought to guarantee regional peace and security through a set of important bilateral alliances rather than through a formal multilateral structure. During the past decade, however, a set of Asian economic structures is starting to emerge that often excludes the United States. To counter this trend and ensure an enduring American role in the region, some have suggested that the United States should seek to formalize regional cooperation into a North East Asia Charter. The United States should not seek formalized cooperation for its own sake, however, particularly if it rewarded parties who do not deserve the benefits of American support. Instead, the next administration should seek to provide regional public goods that increase accountability in areas of common concern, such as on piracy, humanitarian crisis response, or missile early warning.

INTERNATIONAL LEGAL ORDER

For decades, America has been the global champion of international legal norms and standards. This approach not only sought to extend legal protections to others, but also aligned with our self-interest. We knew that our own citizens, military, and corporations needed safeguards abroad. In recent years, however, we have given the impression that America no longer feels bound by these rules that we helped to establish and promote. Many critics see the United States holding countries to a certain set of standards for international conduct that we do not live up to ourselves.

This perception was heightened in the past two decades by the U.S. refusal to ratify a number of treaties that have been embraced by much of the world, including the Convention on the Rights of the Child (193 states party to the convention), the Mine Ban Treaty (ratified by 155 states), the Kyoto Protocol on climate change (ratified by 172 states), and the Rome Statute establishing the International Criminal Court (ratified by 105 states). Although there may have been good reasons for why the United States did not believe these treaties to be in our national interest at the time, the overall message that the United States has sent is one of disregard for the international legal system.

U.S. counterterrorism efforts since 9/11 have furthered the perception that we have abandoned legal norms with respect to interrogation, detention, and rendition. This comes at the very time that we have taken the lead in defining the rule of law as the centerpiece of the world order meant to counter the intolerant vision of terrorists and violent extremists. The images of prisoner abuse from Abu Ghraib probably eroded America's moral authority as much as anything over the past six years because they seemed emblematic of this double standard.

What appears as a double standard abroad is often the product of an ongoing debate within the United States over the place of international law within our domestic legal system. Most Americans would like to conform to international norms, but do not wish to have domestic laws

> "The decision not to sign on to legal frameworks the rest of the world supports is central to the decline in American influence around the world."
>
> SANDRA DAY O'CONNOR

PART II: A SMART POWER STRATEGY   33

that have been written and passed by elected representatives superseded by international institutions over which Americans feel they have little input or control. This is particularly true when Americans perceive their security to be at stake. And yet, the perceived double standard hurts our image and influence with critical allies abroad.

Two principles ought to guide American efforts going forward. The United States directly benefits from a strengthened international legal order. We want our patents to be respected. We want due process when our citizens are held overseas. We want to live in a world where those who commit genocide and crimes against humanity are brought to justice and where the international community finds the will to take action before these horrific crimes occur. A strong international legal order is in America's interests. We ought to take the lead in pursuing those instruments and agreements where an American consensus exists. The Law of the Sea Treaty is one place to start because of the wide support it has garnered from both sides of the aisle.

There will be times, however, when treaties are objectionable because they represent narrow interests or do not provide for a level playing field, or when international legal instruments are ill-prepared to address the challenges of the day. At those times, the United States can justify stepping back, but cannot simply walk away. When serious objections to treaties and legal instruments exist, it is incumbent upon the United States to take the lead in building a new consensus for superior solutions whenever possible.

SIGNATURE INITIATIVE:
INVEST IN A NEW MULTILATERALISM

The United States needs well-functioning international institutions. The next president should prioritize working to reform the United Nations more broadly, reworking the governance structures of the World Bank and International Monetary Fund, and jumpstarting World Trade Organization negotiations and strengthening its enforcement. But beyond these formal structures, we believe that the next president should put energy toward creating a new set of pragmatic groupings to tackle global problems.

The main institutional architecture absent today is an effective forum for coordinating global strategic thinking on a set of specific practical challenges. This is necessary because the crisis-driven nature of the modern world means that governments pay too little attention to envisioning long-range threats, let alone coordinating such thinking with each other. In the absence of shared strategic objectives, crises are more likely to arise that will reverberate throughout the international system. Problems in one country rarely stay within national borders today, and increased integration and interdependence require greater coordination than ever before. In such a world, we need more venues for building common agendas—we need a multilateral pluralism that provides a range of multilateral options for generating new norms and practical solutions to solve global problems.

Currently the Group of Eight (G-8) Summit brings together the governments of Canada, France, Germany, Italy, Japan, Russia, the United

Kingdom, and the United States on a yearly basis to shape a common strategic agenda. Key countries are excluded, however, and to most Americans, the summit appears little more than a talk shop and photo opportunity. The G-8 has made efforts since 2005 to reach out to China, Mexico, India, Brazil, and South Africa as "outreach countries" through a set of ministerial meetings on finance and energy termed the "G-8 + 5." This is a positive step, but it does not go far enough to bring together those governments who can contribute substantively to a whole range of critical challenges.

The next administration should seek to strengthen the G-8 summit process by proposing a set of high-level meetings on those issues routinely addressed by the G-8 that require sustained global attention: energy and climate; nonproliferation; global health; education; and the world economy.

■ Energy Security and Climate. The next administration should take the initiative on seeking a global consensus on how best to address greater resource competition and the potential perils of climate change in the years ahead. The primary objective could be to create a common charter outlining the principles of sound energy policies and practices that could serve as the foundation for global energy security and a healthier environment. The meeting could comprise the world's leading energy consumers and producers—a G-20 group that would account for nearly 80 percent of the world's energy production and consumption. Another option would be an E-8 group that could include four developed blocks (the United States, European Union, Japan, and Russia) and four less-developed (China, India, Brazil, and South Africa) who produce 70 percent of global emissions and yet comprise a small enough group to facilitate productive dialogue. The charter could address issues such as protection of sea lanes and critical infrastructure as well as an investment-friendly regulatory and legal framework that respects the development needs of resource holders.

■ Nonproliferation. The threat of nuclear weapons or material in the hands of terrorists remains the greatest threat facing our country today. This danger may increase as we stand on the forefront of a new boom in the construction of commercial nuclear energy plants. The G-8 summit in Kananaskis in 2002 established a G-8 Global Partnership Against the Spread of Weapons and Materials of Mass Destruction, and the 2006 G-8 summit in St. Petersburg launched a Global Initiative to Combat Nuclear Terrorism. Building on these efforts, the next administration should seek support for an annual high-level meeting on nonproliferation to develop new modes of stemming the transfer of nuclear weapons and materials that could end up in the hands of rogue states or terrorists. The United States ought to encourage China to join us as a key stakeholder in this group.

■ Global Health. Pandemic disease is a transnational threat with the potential to kill more people worldwide than a nuclear attack. Mitigating this threat requires building the public health infrastructure and capacity of first responders around the globe. Doing so will also contribute to the general health of hundreds of millions throughout the developing world. The G-8 has recently focused considerable attention on public health, putting the issue on its agenda for the first time in Okinawa in 2000, endorsing the creation of the Global Health Fund to Fight AIDS, TB, and Malaria at Genoa in 2001, and establishing the Global HIV/AIDS Vaccine Enterprise at the Sea Island summit in 2004. A select group of governments could meet annually to build on these efforts and provide sustained attention and strategic global direction. Membership could be flexible, with aspirants welcome, particularly from Africa, provided they meet entry criteria demonstrating some minimal level of seriousness in engaging on public health.

- Education. Countries with a higher proportion of 15-to-29 year olds relative to the adult population are more likely to descend into armed conflict. Education is the best hope of turning young people away from violence and extremism. But hundreds of millions of children in the developing world are not in school or else attend schools with inadequate teachers or facilities. Since 2000, the G-8 has supported the Education for All Initiative focusing on universal primary school education. An annual high-level meeting could help increase the saliency of U.S. bilateral and multilateral efforts to increase education levels worldwide. Membership could focus on major education donors and recipients. The meeting could also focus on encouraging and harmonizing educational exchanges worldwide.

- World Economy. The world economy is in flux with the growing strength of rising powers in Asia and the convergence of national economic systems. Closer integration means that the ramifications of economic crises in a single sector or country often reverberate throughout the global economy. These changes present new challenges to economic governance committed to free and open markets. An annual G-3 meeting of the United States, Japan, and the European Union, with participation from other emerging economies, could establish norms in corporate governance, regulation, and transparency and seek to identify areas of concern for future growth and stability.

Rather than focus solely on state-to-state interaction, the next administration should take the lead in creating a "Friends Group" for each of the first four meetings that could provide an avenue for key stakeholders in national legislatures, the private sector, and civil society to influence deliberations.

2 GLOBAL DEVELOPMENT

DEVELOPING A MORE UNIFIED APPROACH, STARTING WITH PUBLIC HEALTH

The U.S. commitment and approach to global development has been marked by inconsistency over the past half century. At those times when spending has been successfully justified in terms of American interests—most notably during the Marshall Plan to rebuild post-war Europe, the U.S. government has provided large amounts of aid to foreign lands. For the most part, though, U.S. development policy has lacked a coherent rationale that resonates across departments and agencies of the federal government. If the next administration wants to inspire people in other countries through U.S. assistance, then it will need to develop a more unified approach and convince Americans that smart investments in development are in their own interest.

This lack of coherence is reflected by—and perhaps a product of—the absence of a strong and sustained political basis for global development at home, especially in the absence of an adversary such as the Soviet Union. A number of European nations, in contrast, have strong domestic constituencies for development. To be sure, these have arisen out of their colonial pasts and the realization that development policy allows countries that spend relatively little on military capability to still wield considerable influence, yet many Europeans are ahead of us in realizing that progress around the world is critical for their own stability and prosperity.

Reports of American stinginess have some merit, but can be misleading. Although the United States spends less as a share of its national income than its counterparts in the donor community, it is the largest donor in terms of total dollars spent. American private sector involvement in the developing world—including that of foundations, corporations, voluntary organizations, universities, religious organizations, and individuals through the remittances they send home—typically represents many more times U.S. official government aid on an annual basis. The point here is not that the United States already gives enough official aid and thus should not give more, but that there are many ways that America works for the benefit of the developing world other than through official giving.

Although the amount of foreign aid provided to poor countries sends an important signal of interest and concern, perhaps even more critical is ensuring that the quality of aid makes a real difference in the lives of people it aims to serve. Donor nations have spent hundreds of billions of dollars on development assistance in low- and middle-income countries in recent decades, yet leaders and publics in both recipient and donor countries are still uncertain—and in some cases wary—of the net impact of this effort. Part of the problem stems from the fact that the potential outcomes of foreign aid are long-term, diffuse, and hard to measure. There is no single

PART II: A SMART POWER STRATEGY   37

agreed-upon theory for how to successfully develop a country's economy or lift a population out of poverty.

Another obstacle to effective development assistance is that donor nations do not always share a coordinated approach, much less a common objective, for their money. Many countries even have difficulty coordinating their myriad development programs under one strategic rubric. Aid is used for such divergent goals as spurring economic growth, targeting basic needs, reducing inequalities, strengthening democracy, preventing conflict, or rebuilding countries after war. Foreign assistance frequently has a security imperative that runs counter to development aims. Debt relief and trade liberalization are not always considered as part of an assistance package. Clear strategic direction that guides development policy across the various arms of government—let alone between donor nations—is rare, but remains a critical factor to delivering effective aid.

There have been examples, though, where donors have come together to do impressive things, such as through the Global Fund to Fight AIDS, Tuberculosis, and Malaria. Since 2001, the Global Fund has committed $8.4 billion in 136 countries through an innovative approach to international health financing that brings together governments, civil society, the private sector, and affected communities. The next administration should do more through such multilateral mechanisms.

Poor and corrupt governance on the part of aid recipients also undermines the intended objectives of development aid. Critics of foreign assistance are quick to point to the proverbial money being "poured down a rat hole," whereby the U.S. taxpayer is duped into enriching a small clique of ruling elites at the expense of any long-term institutional development or direct benefit to those abroad. Overcoming this concern remains a significant challenge to building a sustained political constituency for foreign aid in the United States.

The Bush administration and others, however, have made a number of important innovations in global development in the past seven years, perhaps none greater than its effort to take on aid critics' concerns related to poor and corrupt governance. In January 2004, for instance, the administration created the Millennium Challenge Corporation (MCC), a government corporation that delivers foreign aid to poor countries that can demonstrate good governance and a commitment to economic freedom. This new approach, funded through congressional appropriations, has created incentives by which continued aid is tied to good performance.

> "We need a new clarity to our development approach—a clarity of purpose and process, good people, and money on the table to create the trust necessary to work across government and between government and the private sector."
>
> SYLVIA MATHEWS BURWELL

Other laudable programs include President Bush's five-year, $15 billion Emergency Plan for AIDS Relief, or PEPFAR, the largest commitment ever by a country for a health initiative dedicated to a single disease; and the President's Malaria Initiative (PMI), announced in 2005, which earmarks $1.2 billion over five years to cut malaria-related deaths in half in select African nations. The result of these various efforts is that President Bush has tripled overall assistance levels to Africa during his tenure, which in turn has contributed to a favorable opinion of the United States held throughout much of the continent. Figure 4 shows U.S. development and humanitarian assistance funding over the past 20 years. Levels have remained fairly constant for assistance that does not fall under the categories of new initiatives, countries vital to the war on terror, or humanitarian emergencies.

The next president will have to consider which of the Bush administration's development initiatives to sustain, which to expand, and which to take in new directions. Included in this assessment must be an appraisal of the institutional reforms undertaken in recent years. In January 2006, Secretary of State Condoleezza Rice announced the creation of the new position of

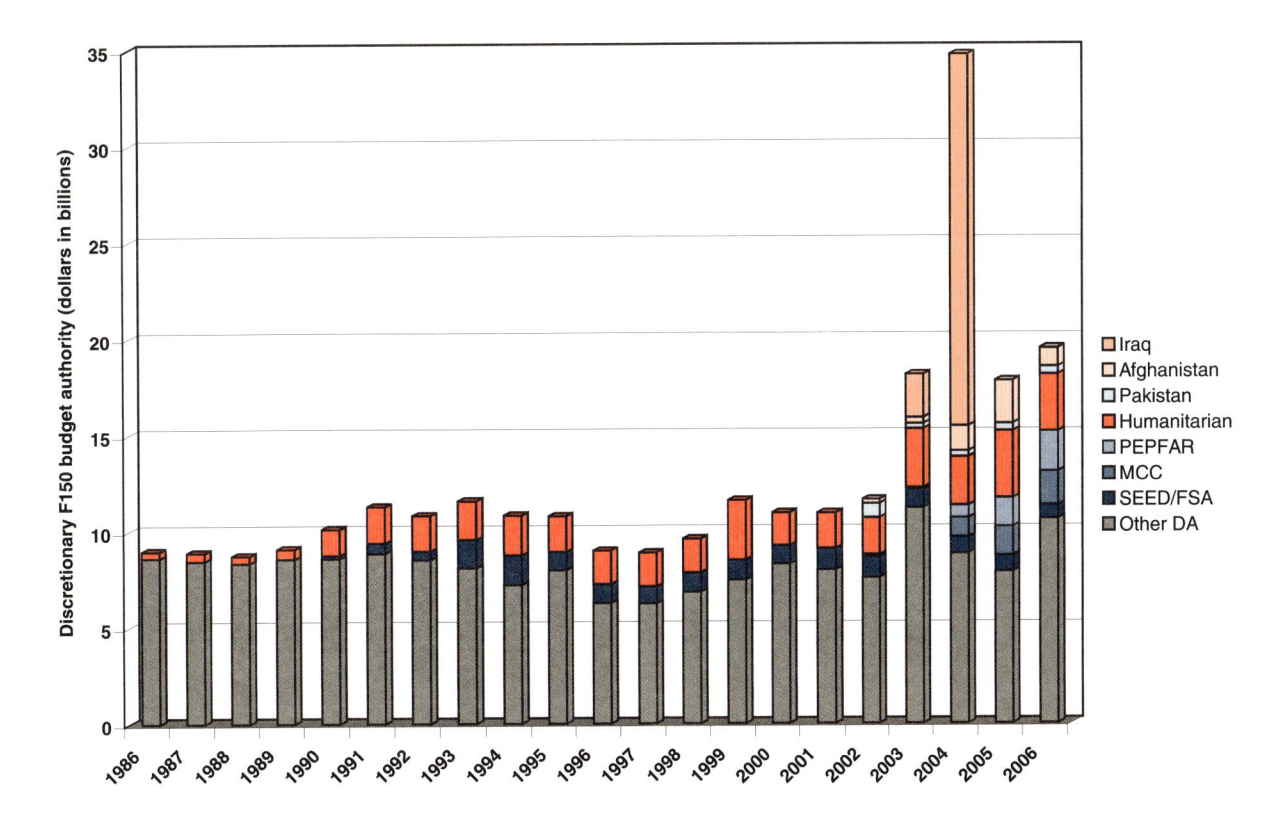

Figure 4. U.S. Development/Humanitarian Assistance Funding, 1986–2006*

*Budget function 150—international affairs only.
Data source: U.S. Office of Management and Budget, public database.

PART II: A SMART POWER STRATEGY   39

director of foreign assistance, who would serve concurrently as USAID administrator at the level of a deputy secretary of state.

The administration's intent was to tie foreign assistance more closely with its transformational diplomacy agenda and America's national interest. Under these reforms, USAID remains an independent organization with an administrator reporting directly to the secretary of state. The director of foreign assistance has the authority over all Department of State and USAID foreign assistance funding and programs, but not those developed in other government agencies, including the Millennium Challenge Corporation, Office of the Global AIDS Coordinator, or the Pentagon. Although the eventual results of these reforms are still too early too tell, few believe they have gone far enough in delivering a unified approach to aid. In particular, the Pentagon's stake in foreign assistance has grown dramatically in the last decade driven by increased authorities in the war on terror (see figure 5).

The main thrust of U.S. global engagement since 9/11 has centered on eliminating the threat of terrorism, and this focus has influenced foreign assistance as well. Secretary Rice sent a clear signal of this when she announced the 2006 reforms, saying that "we must now use our foreign assistance to help prevent future Afghanistans—and to make America and the world safer." Since 9/11, the administration has targeted large amounts of foreign assistance to strategically vital countries in the war on terror, particularly to Iraq, Afghanistan, and Pakistan.

Many in the U.S. development community are deeply concerned that security objectives will overshadow development goals to an even greater extent in this new environment. Although countering the terrorist threat should neither be the overarching tenet of our foreign policy nor of our development assistance, it is difficult to dismiss the counterterrorism rationale for development aid out of hand. As we bring hope to others that they can, by their efforts, improve the quality of their families' lives, they are likely to invest more in their future and be less prone to violence and extremism. In the short term, development also helps to counter the terrorist recruitment narrative that depends not only on a United States that is weak-willed, but on an America that is hard-hearted. Today's central question is not simply whether we are capturing or killing more terrorists than are being recruited and trained, but whether we are providing more opportunities than our enemies can destroy and whether we are addressing more grievances than they can record.

> Today's central question is not simply whether we are capturing or killing more terrorists than are being recruited and trained, but whether we are providing more opportunities than our enemies can destroy and whether we are addressing more grievances than they can record.

Although development aid will continue to be used to counter security threats, any increase in assistance levels ought to be spread more purposefully throughout the world, rather than merely in three strategic countries or one strategic region. What is paramount is the signal America sends globally—that we want the world to share in our prosperity, and we want our aid to address local aspirations. This depends on the United States' placing a greater priority on listening.

The most sustainable rationale for global development over time is this: American leaders ought to commit to global development because it reinforces basic American values, contributes to peace, justice, and prosperity, and improves the way we are viewed around the world. Investing in development contributes to American security at home by promoting stability abroad.

In today's world, creating conditions where people around the world can realize their own aspirations

Figure 5. U.S. Department of Defense–funded International Assistance Activities, 1997–2006*

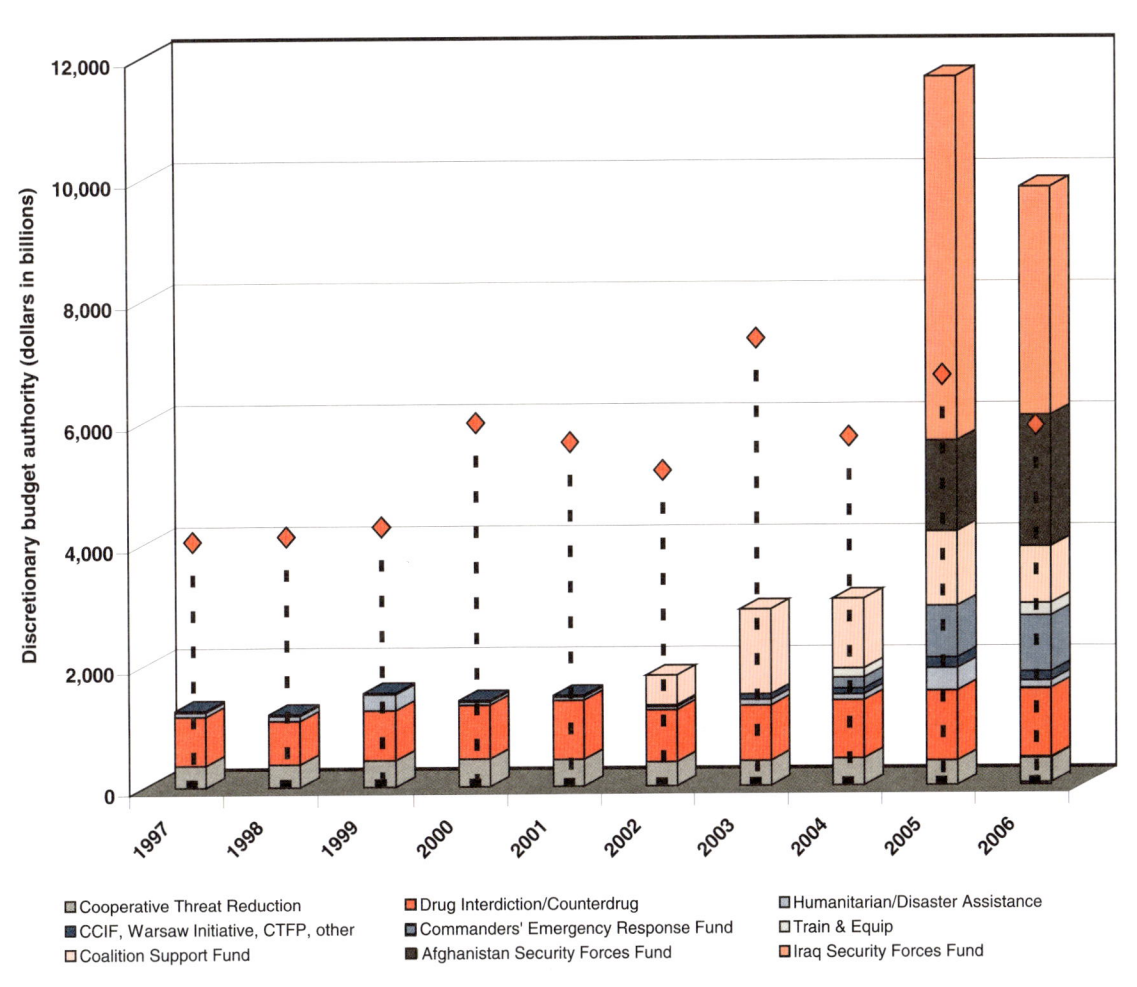

- Cooperative Threat Reduction
- Drug Interdiction/Counterdrug
- Humanitarian/Disaster Assistance
- CCIF, Warsaw Initiative, CTFP, other
- Commanders' Emergency Response Fund
- Train & Equip
- Coalition Support Fund
- Afghanistan Security Forces Fund
- Iraq Security Forces Fund

◆ · · · ◆ F150 Military/Narcotics/Law enforcement/Antiterrorism/Nonproliferation compared.

*Budget function 050—defense/military only.
Data sources: U.S. Office of Management and Budget, public database; U.S. Department of Defense, Congressional Budget Justifications, FY 1999–2008; U.S. Department of Defense Appropriations Acts, Committee and Conference Reports, FY 2002–2006.
Note: CCIF = Combatant Commander Initiatives Fund; CTFP = Counterterrorism Fellowship Program.

is of strategic importance. This is true in more parts of the world than merely countries that are home to terrorists or extremist ideologies. Investing in development makes it more likely that governments and citizens will take decisions to stand by America's side when we need allies most. It is not that people around the world will automatically form their opinions of the United States based on our aid rather than our policies, nor that the United States should spend development money in order to "get people to like us." But how America spends its money overseas reflects our priorities, and people overseas realize this. Greater support to the UN Millennium Development Goals (MDGs)—launched in 2000 with the purpose of achieving concrete, measurable progress toward alleviating hunger and poverty and improving education and health by 2015 around the world—could help in this regard.

In the short run, the next president will need to address three vital development issues in the brief window of opportunity that exists at the beginning of any new administration: elevating the development mission within the U.S. government; developing a more unified approach to our aid; and developing locally supported and measurable delivery systems.

Elevating the development mission. In practice, this means that the next administration should continue the Bush administration's efforts to increase the size of the development and humanitarian assistance budget and increase the effectiveness of this assistance. The next administration should also create a cabinet-level voice for global development, a recommendation expanded upon in the final section of this report on implementation. There are internal and external reasons for such a move. Internally, a cabinet-level voice could bring greater coherence across the aid community and the entire U.S. foreign policy establishment and provide a sense of common purpose for development personnel in the U.S. government. Retention, recruitment, and training of experienced development staff are currently major challenges. Externally, a cabinet-level voice for global development would show a different American face to the world. Development is a theme that aligns America with the world's less fortunate and cements international partnerships.

A more unified approach. More than 50 separate units of the U.S. government are currently pursuing more than 50 foreign assistance objectives. The Bush administration was right to launch a foreign assistance reform process in 2006 to streamline budgeting and planning and increase transparency. What is needed, however, is not just a new framework for USAID, but one that could be put into operational practice across all departments and agencies of the U.S. government and could help prioritize strategic objectives and direct resources. The UK's Department for International Development (DFID), for instance, leads on trade policy in developing countries and meets weekly with the military's Joint Chiefs of Staff. In the United States, though, turf trumps transformation.

Experts have suggested various institutional models to promote integration of planning, programming, and evaluation to update the coordinated, decentralized U.S. model. Alternatives include making USAID an implementing arm of the State Department (such as in Norway and Sweden), merging USAID into the State Department (such as in the Netherlands, Finland, and Denmark), creating a Department for Global Development (such as in the UK and Canada), appointing a development "czar," or else undertaking a major restructuring and creating a Department of Foreign Affairs that would bring all assistance programs of the International Affairs Budget (150 account) into one department. The next administration will have to determine which institutional configuration is most fitting for a global power and most likely to get congressional support. Whatever the next president decides, he or she should take action to build greater coherence for America's development assistance.

Locally supported delivery systems. The next administration should also place a greater effort on making American aid more effective by working with local civil society and private sector actors to invest in more agile, innovative, and locally supported delivery systems. There is a reason that groups like Hamas and Hezbollah provide effective assistance. Although their goals run counter to U.S. interests, these groups are rooted in local communities, have relatively little overhead and corruption, and rely on a network-based rather than a bureaucratic approach.

International nongovernmental organizations (NGOs) have an important role to play in delivering aid, particularly when local partners on the ground lack the capacity to manage large projects, but rural development networks may prove to be better partners than U.S. contractors or even local NGOs that sprout up overnight in the capital with few constituents and perfect English-language skills. This may require reassessing the regulations on partner organizations.

It may also require increased oversight capacity within government aid agencies. The next administration should spend money on innovative methods of measuring outcomes through reliable metrics. Aid agencies should develop new metrics for success that incorporate attitudinal research in conjunction with local partners.

A renewed commitment to global development means strengthening relationships with international and domestic partners and trying to build a more unified approach at home and abroad. As a first priority, the next administration should start with the dynamic and growing field of global health, which affects every person in every nation and is an area that permits the United States to provide assistance without appearing to have a hidden agenda.

SIGNATURE INITIATIVE:
BUILD A GLOBAL HEALTH NETWORK

As discussed above, the next administration will need to quickly address a number of fundamental big picture questions about how our development assistance is organized. Until this occurs, it is difficult to comprehensively address any of the issue baskets that will eventually constitute a development approach, such as poverty alleviation, education assistance, or health. And yet, designing a new approach in any of these areas could demonstrate an institutional model for going forward.

> "Global health is more than just a medical issue. It is fundamental to everything America wants for the world."
>
> HELENE D. GAYLE

Health is vital to development. It is also vital for human and national security, for economic growth, and for building stable ties between countries. It is fundamental to every family's livelihood and existence. As mentioned earlier in this report, U.S. leadership on global health has expanded in recent years, drawing on both the public and private sectors, and has made significant progress in battling HIV/AIDS and malaria, particularly in Africa. Yet many countries lack the systems and infrastructure to make effective use of the funds and to deliver broader health outcomes. Working with international partners, including the United Nations, the next administration should expand upon the Bush administration's legacy and look beyond a single-disease approach to work with countries and across regions to build integrated health systems that can significantly reduce gross health inequities borne today by the world's poor.

The United States should create new venues to align strategy and resources on global health, domestically and internationally. The next administration should seek to strengthen leadership networks, improve planning capacity, and foster coordination between government health ministries and civil society to bring greater coherence to global health efforts. New leadership from the top, however, will prove ineffective without increased capacity at the local level. The next administration should also make new investments in the training of local health care providers abroad.

New leadership, planning, and coordination are necessary within the U.S. government as well. It is essential that we marshal diverse experts in national security, public health, and economic development from the public and private sectors behind a long-term, unified vision for global public health and that government officials operate within a better coordinated institutional architecture.

The next administration should mandate coordination and leadership of global health efforts in a new subcabinet position, provided this fits with the overall institutional architecture to build greater policy coherence within the U.S. government. One of the problems with our development institutions generally, and with our health efforts specifically, is that they lack a national focus that makes sense for our international role and that could guide our efforts over the long term. A national focus could raise the importance of health and development more broadly within the federal bureaucracy, where knowledge on health and development is thin and where decisionmakers often view health as a niche issue rather than one that cuts across national security, trade, and diplomacy.

■ Create a U.S. Global Health Corporation (GHC). A main imperative of the next administration should be to build a more unified approach to development and health. Creating yet another new organization such as the GHC could undermine this goal, yet there is always a trade-off between building the required institutional capacity to address a vital issue (despite the risk of reducing coherence, flexibility, and local ownership) and working within existing structures that may not be up to the job. Furthermore, the Millennium Challenge Corporation model is unique in many ways and not the appropriate institutional answer for every development challenge. A GHC, however, could better respond to the looming strategic challenges ahead in global health, such as the health workforce deficit, that go beyond traditional mandates.

Specifically, it could help strengthen institutional health capacity overseas by dramatically expanding the availability of skilled doctors and nurses in the developing world. Doctors and nurses are the foot soldiers in the war against sickness and disease. The estimated global health care worker shortage now stands at more than 4 million. The GHC could work with regional partners to create new training centers for health care professionals and seek to reach a workable compact with developing countries to reduce the commercial recruitment of newly trained talent away from their home countries.

The GHC could also take the lead toward a renewed focus on maternal and children's health. Millions of children around the world die every year from preventable death. Prenatal care, nutrition, vaccinations, clean water, and basic parental health education could save countless lives. Improving child and maternal health contributes to both poverty reduction and economic development. The GHC could function as an independent corporation with a board of governors charged with global health and include senior officials from the Center for Disease Control, the National Institute of Health, Congress, foundations, NGOs, medical professionals, health researchers, and the health care industry.

■ Strengthen the leadership of the World Health Organization (WHO). The WHO, the UN's health arm, is the natural leader on public health, but lacks the budget, governance, and staffing to command attention in the event of a global pandemic. The ultimate aim should be to transform the WHO into a truly leading global agency able to set new norms and standards for global health, produce cutting-edge analysis to guide international action in the future, and spearhead the creation of new global surveillance and response capabilities for emerging pandemics. In this way, the United States could show its commitment to addressing development through multilateral institutions. The next administration should seek to convince not just the core G-8 members of the wisdom of this goal, but also to enlist China, India, Brazil, and others in the developing world in the effort. Reform and rejuvenation of the WHO should be tied to a few new strategic global initiatives that will bring broad and concrete benefits, such as the surveillance and control of pandemics, or dealing with shared problems of chronic diseases and long-term effects of obesity, tobacco, and alcohol abuse.

- Bring safe drinking water and sanitation to every person in the world. The scarcity of safe drinking water is reaching crisis proportions. The WHO estimates that more than 1 billion people lack access to clean water. Water insecurity could potentially threaten security and stability in key regions in the years ahead. Providing clean water and working sanitation could help prevent disease and prolong life. Providing potable water for all people across the globe is an achievable and relatively inexpensive endeavor—if we have the leadership to tackle it. One of the MDGs focuses on water, aiming to cut in half the percentage of people without access to safe water by 2015. This goal is supported by the Water for the Poor Act, which President Bush signed in 2005—the first time an MDG was written into U.S. law. The next administration should launch a new U.S. development initiative to spur the integration of innovations in both development policy and technology, in cooperation with multilateral and community-based partners and private organizations. The costs of purifying water are falling due to emerging technologies, and the U.S. government could launch a concerted effort to bring these to areas of priority need. The U.S. government should expand its funding for both large-scale and small-scale community-based water and sanitation efforts in developing countries.

- End the stigma of AIDS at home and abroad. The United States is making historic investments in fighting HIV/AIDS around the world, including in Africa, but the stigma attached to the disease remains strong. More research and programming should be devoted to innovative ways of encouraging voluntary testing and treatment, despite existing inhibitions, as well as to prevention and the development of a vaccine. The next administration should make the same efforts at home. In particular, under current U.S. law and policy, HIV infection is grounds for denying admission of non-citizens—immigrants and non-immigrants alike—to the United States. Although waivers are available on a case-by-case basis, this law, which was put in place more than 20 years ago, is outdated and sends an inconsistent, even hostile message. The next president has the opportunity to end a policy that goes against good public health practices, furthers the stigma associated with HIV and AIDS, and undermines American leadership on health and beyond.

3 PUBLIC DIPLOMACY

IMPROVING ACCESS TO INTERNATIONAL KNOWLEDGE AND LEARNING

Effective public diplomacy is central to any discussions about American image and influence in the world today. The intent of public diplomacy is to communicate with the people, not the governments, of foreign countries. Governments traditionally use public diplomacy to exercise influence over individuals, groups, institutions, and public opinion abroad in support of their national objectives. Public diplomacy is broader, though, than the official activities of government. It is part-and-parcel of everything America does and says as a country and society. Every U.S. citizen serves as a diplomat, whether at home interacting with foreigners or when traveling abroad.

Recent U.S. administrations have struggled to get public diplomacy right. More than public relations, effective public diplomacy moves both people and information and helps provide insight into the policies and values of the United States. It also improves Americans' awareness and understanding of the world beyond our shores. Despite past successes during the Cold War, many U.S. decisionmakers dismiss public diplomacy as ineffective or as mere propaganda. Although a number of independent commissions have criticized the U.S. government for problems implementing public diplomacy, it remains a critical part of U.S. smart power.

Much of the current debate over revitalizing public diplomacy efforts has centered on institutional arrangements and resource levels. It is a well-known story by now that during the Cold War, the U.S. Information Agency (USIA) undertook public diplomacy and helped to shape public opinion behind the Iron Curtain. In the Cold War's aftermath, however, the United States essentially demobilized its public diplomacy efforts as part of a budget-cutting "peace dividend." Beginning in 1995, Congress drastically cut funding for the activities of the USIA, which the Clinton administration eventually merged into the State Department in 1999.

Although the Clinton administration created a new under secretary for public diplomacy in 1999 and overall spending on information and educational and cultural affairs rebounded in 2001 under the Bush administration, spending has remained at levels well below the USIA budgets at the start of the 1990s. Current annual public diplomacy spending is just under $1.5 billion—comparable to what France and Britain each spend annually on public diplomacy efforts.

> "A smarter public diplomacy is one that shows respect toward other countries and a willingness to understand local needs and local issues."
>
> JOHN ZOGBY

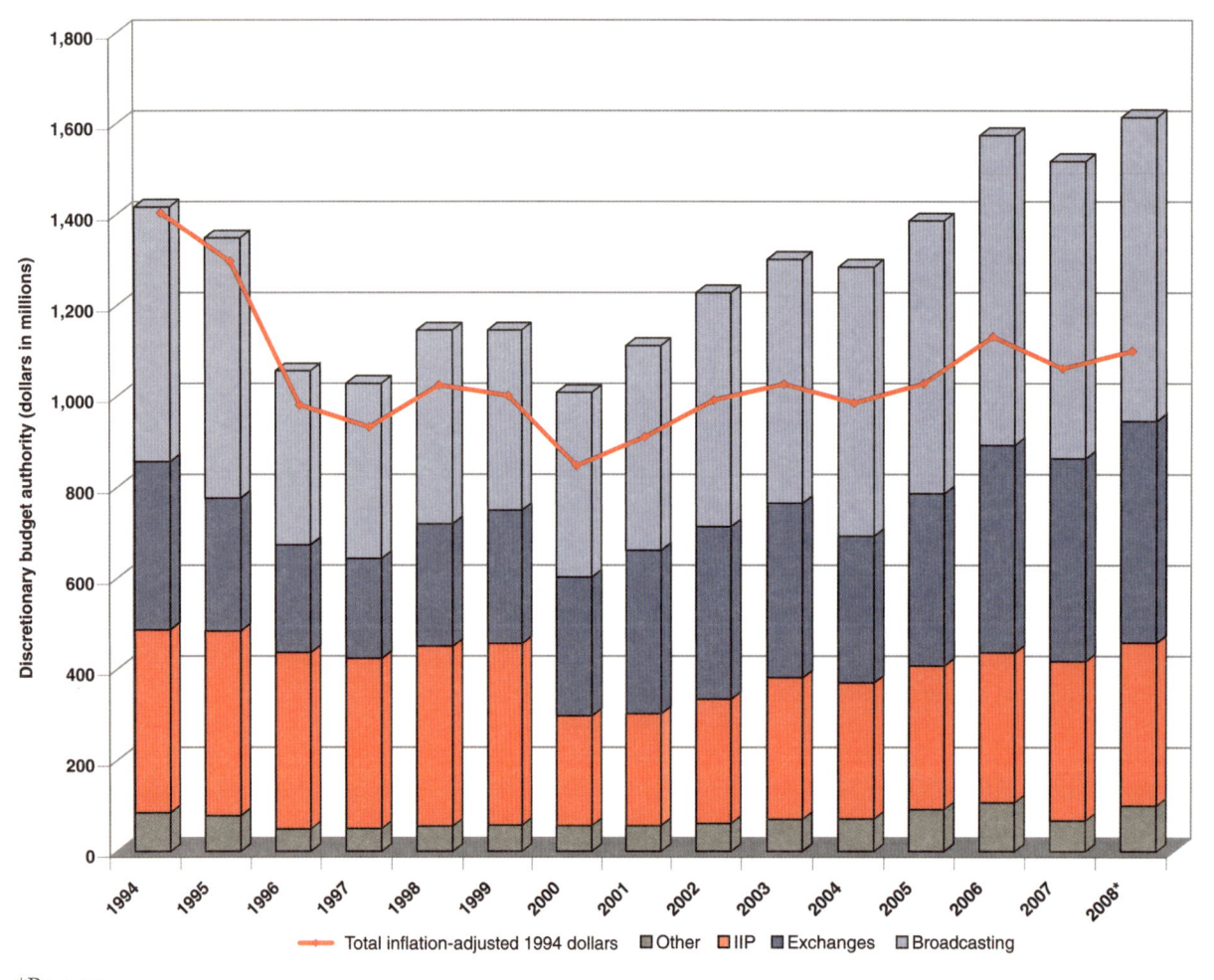

Figure 6. Public Diplomacy Spending, 1994–2008

*Request
Data source: U.S. Office of Management and Budget, public database.

Note: IIP = International Information Programs; other = (principally) National Endowment for Democracy, East-West Center, Asia Foundation, and North-South Center.

Figure 6 shows the past 15 years of U.S. spending on public diplomacy.

Although USIA should not have been abolished, reviving the agency may not be the most practical option at present. The next administration should strengthen our resource commitment to public diplomacy and consider what institutional remedies—in addition to capable leadership—could help make U.S. government public diplomacy efforts work most effectively. One possibility the next administration should consider is the establishment of an autonomous organization charged with public diplomacy and reporting directly to the secretary of state. This quasi-independent entity would be responsible for the full range of

48 CSIS COMMISSION ON SMART POWER

government public diplomacy initiatives, including those formerly conducted by USIA.

Whatever the institutional framework, improving the effectiveness of U.S. government public diplomacy efforts in the field will require a higher degree of cultural understanding and awareness on the part of American officials. Local populations often discount U.S. government public diplomacy efforts as official propaganda because these efforts fail to be properly situated in the local context. Little will change if diplomats are penned in by embassy walls and lack adequate resources or if broadcasting misreads cultural cues and appears to be inauthentic, as is too often the case.

CSIS recently addressed this issue through another high-level commission. The Commission on the Embassy of the Future defined "embassy" in a broad sense, of which embassy buildings are only one dimension. U.S. presence and diplomatic capacity are functions first and foremost of our people and their ability to carry out their mission.

The Embassy of the Future Commission supported the modernization and reform of the diplomatic profession and its infrastructure that are already under way. It urged the State Department to do more, however, including building a bigger and better-trained State Department workforce, embracing the technology and policies that can expand diplomatic reach, and implementing a risk-managed approach to security that allows for greater interactions in the field required for successful diplomatic engagement.

Certain elements of public diplomacy will always remain in the government's purview since it is linked to the national interest and policy objectives of the U.S. government, and individuals and groups who do not share or understand these objectives cannot effectively carry forth the government's message. The U.S. government, though, may not always be the best entity to engage foreign populations in public diplomacy. Today's environment poses new challenges to U.S. public diplomacy efforts. Most governments are used to speaking with a single, authoritative voice to other governments. They control their message and counter misinformation through traditional diplomatic methods and channels. The advent of the global information age and a growing and highly fractured political consciousness, however, have increased the difficulty of favorably shaping public opinion in foreign lands. Attacks on America's message from non-state actors can only be countered with an agility and authenticity that most governments lack.

Nongovernmental organizations have a role to play in strategic communication, provided that they are viewed as genuinely independent organizations not necessarily toeing the official line. The final chapter of this report recommends that the next administration create an institution outside of government that could help tap into expertise in the private and nonprofit sectors to improve U.S. strategic communication from an outside-in approach. The following signature initiative picks up on this theme, suggesting new U.S. government investments in citizen diplomacy.

SIGNATURE INITIATIVE:
INVEST IN EDUCATIONAL EXCHANGES

Public diplomacy efforts go well beyond USIA, the Voice of America, and other media-driven approaches. An effective public diplomacy approach must include exchanges of ideas, peoples, and information through person-to-person educational and cultural exchanges, often referred to as citizen diplomacy. Years of successful exchanges have demonstrated the effectiveness of face-to-face interactions in breaking through stereotypes and creating trust. As Edward R. Murrow famously said, the critical link in the international communication chain is the "last three feet," which is bridged by personal contact. In this regard, the American public constitutes the United States' greatest public diplomacy assets, particularly young people who increasingly study, work, volunteer, and travel overseas.

Today's youth are perhaps the most globally aware generation in history. More than any other age cohort today, they consider themselves to be "citizens of the planet Earth" rather than citizens of the United States. They tend to favor a wiser internationalism and have a sense that their actions have impact far beyond their own community. Nearly one in four expect to study, live, or work in another country during their lifetime. The number of U.S. college students studying abroad as part of their college experience has doubled over the last decade to more than 200,000, though this still represents slightly more than 1 percent of all American undergraduates enrolled in public, private, and community institutions.

One way to encourage U.S. citizen diplomacy is to strengthen and expand America's study abroad programs at both the university and high school levels. The typical American student who studies abroad today is a white woman from a middle or upper class background, pursuing a liberal arts degree and studying for eight weeks or less in England or another country in Western Europe.

In addition to increasing the number of American students going abroad, the next administration should make it a priority to increase the number of international students coming to the United States for study and research and to better integrate them into campus life. Some Americans may be wary of opening our doors during war time, particularly to students from the Arab and Muslim world, but these students pose less of a security threat than other foreign nationals in the United States. They are now the most closely monitored and can provide our society with the greatest benefit.

America remains the world's leading education destination, with more than a half-million international students in the country annually. Numerous surveys show that the best and brightest are

> "The American education system is the foundation of good public diplomacy and our international image."
>
> ALLAN E. GOODMAN

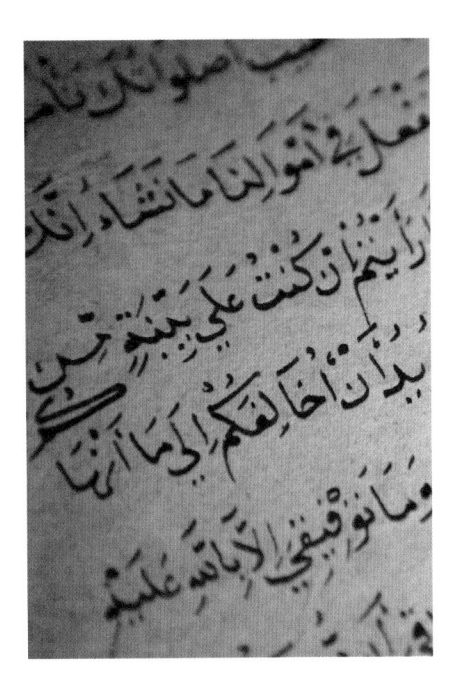

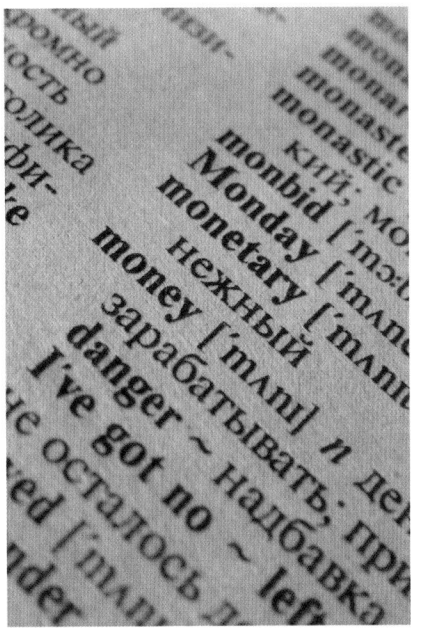

attracted by the quality and diversity of our educational system, the degree of innovation and choice it permits, and our historically open academic doors. Interest in the nation's Fulbright exchange program is at record high levels, and applications have substantially increased since immediately after 9/11, including from the Islamic world.

Despite these positive trends, however, many foreign students looking for educational opportunities have turned away from the United States, in part because of the perception that America has become less hospitable to foreigners. Although student visas are no longer the problem they once were, border inspections and homeland security requirements remain unnecessarily onerous and unwelcoming. There was once a time when Americans could assume with some degree of certainty that many of the future leaders of foreign countries would be educated in the United States. This may no longer be the case.

We urge the next president of the United States to make educational and institutional exchanges a higher priority by taking the following steps.

- Expand successful exchange and education programs. In 2006, the U.S. Department of State spent $238.4 million on academic exchanges, of which $183.9 million was attributable to the Fulbright program. Congress should double this appropriation, with greater emphasis placed on support for students and professionals in the medical, engineering, computer sciences, and education field. The next administration should also expand the State Department's International Visitor Leadership Program, which has welcomed more than 200 current and former heads of government, and the Department of Defense's National Security Education Program, which provides opportunities for U.S. students to become more proficient in cultures and languages of world regions critical to U.S. interests.

PART II: A SMART POWER STRATEGY   51

- Launch U.S.-China and U.S.-India Educational Funds. China and India are rising powers and together compose more than a third of the world's population. The next administration should propose a ten-year special allocation of new funds administered through the Fulbright program to create a new generation of American specialists on China and India, as well as a new generation of Chinese and Indian specialists on the United States.

- Expand Middle East language competencies. Since 9/11, there has been a substantial increase in American students studying Arabic and other languages of the Middle East and Southwest Asia, but more are needed. During the Cold War, the U.S. government funded programs to build an intellectual foundation for understanding the Soviet Union in our colleges and universities and to teach relevant language skills. The commission believes the U.S. government should increase spending to boost scholarships and language competencies relevant to the broader Middle East.

- Draw on America's cultural advantages. America's immigrant communities provide a rich source of international understanding within our borders. Many Americans have a connection to other parts of the world, are fluent in their ancestral language, and could serve as citizen diplomats abroad. Too few of these people take part in exchange programs or are accepted into civilian service within the U.S. government. The U.S. government's security paranoia discourages Americans of foreign background from holding national security positions. With proper monitoring and screening, the next administration should consider these Americans to be security assets rather than security risks. The U.S government should provide financial incentives, such as tuition assistance, for first-generation Americans to work in foreign policy or national security positions in the U.S. government.

> "America will be a smarter and stronger power as we draw more fully on the rich diversity of our society."
>
> TERENCE A. TODMAN

4 ECONOMIC INTEGRATION

INCREASING THE BENEFITS OF TRADE FOR ALL PEOPLE

In this period of accelerating global economic integration, with all the opportunities and challenges that it implies, America stands as one of the most critical players on the world stage. The United States is the world's largest economy, the largest exporter and importer, and the recipient of the greatest amount of foreign direct investment. The American labor force is highly flexible and productive, and our corporate and financial structures are world class.

International trade has been a critical ingredient to U.S. economic growth and prosperity. Over the past decade, trade has helped increase U.S. gross domestic product by nearly 40 percent, resulting in net job creation in the United States. Approximately one-fifth of American jobs depend on trade. Manufacturing exports have increased 82 percent over the past decade, and one in every three U.S. acres is used to produce products or services for export. Trade also ensures that American consumers have access to affordable goods and services. It helps keep inflation in check, interest rates low, and investment levels high. In recent years, it also helped dampen the effects of recession when the U.S. economy has slowed.

The United States is inextricably tied to the global economy that we took the lead in building in the aftermath of World War II. We are also possibly the nation that benefits most from trade. Because the United States has an open economy, with tariffs and nontariff measures among the lowest in the world, further global trade liberalization through the World Trade Organization (WTO) or free trade agreements means that other nations are required to reduce their barriers to trade proportionately more than we must ourselves. Put simply, the United States is a net winner in the international trade system.

This reality should not breed complacency, however. The United States must do more to prepare itself for increasing economic competition. American entrepreneurs and companies no longer dominate the realm of new ideas and products. For example, half of all patents issued in 2006 were of foreign origin. American contributions to scientific journals have declined by more than 15 percent in the past 15 years. In 1981, U.S. national security institutions accounted for one-fifth of research and development among developed countries, but today that fraction has declined to roughly one-tenth. American excellence in science and technology underlies the nation's economic performance, quality of life, and national security.

The changing nature of the global economy has fundamentally altered the basis of global

"Trade is an opportunity to compete and make a better world for all people."

CHUCK HAGEL

> "Fifty years ago the federal government was the main decisionmaker. Now, the private sector and individuals have a much greater ability to drive policy."
>
> DAVID M. RUBENSTEIN

competition. Unlike in the past, the competition is less for markets and more for capital, talent, and ideas. For example, the changes in computing, communications, and transport technology have made the operation of a global supply chain a competitive necessity.

To ensure that we have the best talent and ideas, the next administration must reexamine our public school system to ensure that we are graduating high school students ready for work, college, and citizenship. The Bush administration has admirably sought to do this through No Child Left Behind, but a regular reassessment of how and what our young people are learning is critical. Whether a high school graduate goes on to higher education or not, he or she will enter a workplace that is most likely tied to the global economy.

The American private sector also has a responsibility to help educate the next generation of workers. The next president should challenge the corporate sector to develop its own training and internship programs that could help teach the skills that American workers will need in the decades to come. The next administration should consider a tax credit for companies to make their in-house training available to public schools and community colleges.

Companies should also remain actively involved in pushing for a more effective immigration policy. Although immigration is not the subject of this commission, in our aging society, immigrants are central to maintaining American economic productivity, competitiveness, and job growth. The next administration should seek to build bipartisan consensus on a smart immigration policy that takes advantage of immigrant skills at both the high and low ends of the employment ladder.

There is no doubt that the benefits of trade are not evenly distributed—within a nation or across nations. There is growing anxiety both within the United States and around the world about whether the global economic system can work for all. This anxiety finds its political expression in a growing economic populism that openly questions the benefits of trade and has an instinct to withdraw from global engagement. Although the current administration has supported the expansion of free trade, many in Congress are calling for a halt to new trade agreements, the rollback of existing accords like NAFTA, and higher barriers to immigration.

> The American private sector also has a responsibility to help educate the next generation of workers.

Anxiety about the global economy is not limited to the United States, nor is it new. For decades, political leaders across the globe have appealed to local populist sentiment and opposed greater economic integration. Today—whether it is the near collapse of the Doha Round of the WTO, battles in Europe over the European Constitution, failed attempts to create a Free Trade Agreement of the Americas, or delays in concluding bilateral free trade agreements—efforts to tie economies closer together continue to come under question and under fire.

The answer to competition should not be retrenchment but further engagement—and the United States must take the lead. Americans have never shied away from a tough fight. Rather, we have responded by honing our skills and staying on the cutting edge. It should be no different today. However, as we embrace healthy competition, we must also not forget those who lose their jobs or are displaced by globalization. Current data and analysis illustrate that the gains from globalization are disproportionately concentrated at the upper end of the income distribution chain with earnings among the middle class falling. The middle class continues to be disproportionately affected by the economic changes under way in the American economy, including the impact of globalization.

Easing the burden on U.S. and foreign workers most affected by globalization is an essential part of an effective global trade strategy. Politicians should support domestic economic policies that foster a broader sharing of the benefits of global engagement. Trade Adjustment Assistance, despite its recent expansion, has met with mixed reviews. Its objectives are the right ones, though—helping displaced workers develop new skills and transfer into new industries. More must be done on this front.

Internationally, the next president must refocus U.S. foreign assistance as this report previously discussed and, to the extent possible, exercise U.S. influence in international financial institutions to direct the efforts of these organizations toward aiding poorer countries that face the inevitable adjustment issues that come with an opening of markets. We should also reexamine our own trade policies toward these nations. An interesting model could be the EU's "Everything but Arms" regime for the least-developed nations, which provides for tariff-free access to all goods other than arms, including most agricultural products. It is in the U.S. interest to ensure that those hurt most by globalization—our world's poorest nations and people—are able to make new lives for themselves. Conversely, it is against our economic and security interests to contribute to or ignore poverty and desperation around the world.

A smarter global trade policy depends on shaping an economy that is sufficiently flexible and

> The answer to competition should not be retrenchment but further engagement—and the United States must take the lead.

competitive enough to deliver economic benefits while minimizing the human cost of adjusting to economic dislocation. This is a bipartisan challenge and must be a bipartisan effort.

SIGNATURE INITIATIVE:
RELAUNCH THE DOHA ROUND ON MORE EQUITABLE TERMS

■ Create a Free Trade Core within the WTO. The next administration should negotiate a "plurilateral" agreement among those WTO members willing to move directly to free trade on a global basis. The objective of the core, which would have a defined process and accession criteria, would be to provide a more effective alternative to the proliferation of bilateral free trade agreements outside the WTO, which are proceeding apace and in some cases undermining the multilateral framework. Although consensus within the full WTO would be the ideal and should remain the goal, it is in many cases not realistic. A core group would restore the cause of liberalization within the WTO and might even prod those who resist liberalization closer toward free trade. Countries not able or willing to meet the core criteria would be allowed to observe the talks, from which they are specifically excluded at bilateral and multilateral trade negotiations.

■ Lock in a Minimum Measure of Global Trade Liberalization. Negotiate a fully multilateral round of trade liberalization applicable to all WTO member countries based on the limited commitments already on the table in the Doha Round.

■ Free Market Access for the Least-Developed Countries. Developed countries should follow the EU lead and offer free market access without reciprocity to the poorest nations. The United States should encourage middle income developing countries and other emerging markets, such as Brazil, Russia, India, China, and South Africa, to develop a harmonized schedule for doing the same.

■ Recommit to Facilitating Adjustment. To help displaced workers at home, the next administration and Congress should fundamentally reform Trade Adjustment Assistance (TAA) in the United States. It should be combined with the resources of unemployment insurance and Workforce Investment Act programs into a single government program designed to facilitate the reentry of American workers who lose their jobs, regardless of whether the loss can be tied to trade.

■ Challenge the Private Sector to Maintain Best Practices. The onus of ensuring that workers around the world have the same rights as workers in the United States is on our corporate leadership. It hurts America's image and influence for U.S. companies to take advantage of workers in poor countries simply to boost an already strong bottom line. Many American companies understand and honor this code, but not all. American corporate leaders ought to speak out publicly on this issue.

5 TECHNOLOGY AND INNOVATION

ADDRESSING CLIMATE CHANGE AND ENERGY INSECURITY

Enhancing our energy security must become more than a political catch phrase. It requires concerted action and policies aimed at reducing demand through improved efficiency, diversifying energy suppliers and fuel choices, and managing geopolitics in resource-rich areas that currently account for the majority of our imports. The importance of finding creative solutions is only likely to intensify in the years ahead.

Over the coming decade, world energy demand is projected to rise to unprecedented levels driven by population growth and economic development. A growing proportion of this demand growth will occur in developing countries, particularly China and India. Massive amounts of investment and infrastructure will be required to produce and deliver enough energy to meet these societies' needs.

Limitations to developing oil and gas resources, the majority of which are geographically concentrated in a handful of regions, are driving greater concern over energy security in various regions around the globe. This in turn is spurring development of new energy resources and creating incentives for a greater reliance on domestically abundant resources like coal in the United States, China, and India. This remarkable growth in demand is occurring at a time when a patchwork of carbon-constrained environments has emerged in response to increasing concern over the impact of global climate change.

In response, American states and cities as well as countries around the world and a growing portion of the private sector are taking action to reduce their respective greenhouse gas emissions (GHGs) while simultaneously calling for greater commitments on the part of the U.S. government and other major rising emitters like China

> "Powering the global economy, creating millions of new jobs, and keeping our planet alive and healthy should be a national priority."
>
> BETTY McCOLLUM

> "Innovation and creativity are our inherent national strengths and must be harnessed to meet the great challenges facing America today."
>
> NANCY LANDON KASSEBAUM BAKER

and India. Both the U.S. government and industry are increasingly responding to these trends.

In the past year, there has been increasing awareness of how countries and companies view their own energy production and use, as well as their environmental footprint. For instance, a July 2007 study by the National Petroleum Council (NPC), which represents the major oil and gas industry perspective, was entitled *Hard Truths: Facing the Hard Truths about Energy* and stressed the importance of energy efficiency and the development of alternative fuels as part of a multi-component approach. New innovation on energy and climate is being spurred by state and local regulations and company anticipation of government regulation on a national level.

Many companies are delaying investment in a variety of energy infrastructure projects, however, particularly in the power generation sector. This is because of uncertainty over the sustained traction of climate policies emerging at the state and local level and questions of whether and how soon affordable technology for providing low-carbon alternatives will come online. Companies also are uncertain over the cost and regulatory approach associated with implementing carbon constraints, as well as the risk of the emergence of future constraints. This delay in investment in infrastructure undermines the reliability of our current energy supply.

A world operating on differing sets of rules or costs associated with carbon dioxide emissions could have disruptive implications for trade, energy security, competitiveness, and economic growth. A world, however, that establishes a global consensus on the cost of carbon could breathe life into new and emerging sectors of the economy, provide new avenues for U.S. economic growth, and provide a platform for U.S. global leadership on a major issue of concern to the global economy.

U.S. leadership to shape a new energy framework in a carbon-constrained world offers a unique opportunity to alter the geopolitics of energy, improve energy security, reinvigorate the spirit of innovation and entrepreneurialism, and engage disenfranchised portions of the developing world.

A smart power approach to energy security and climate should focus on what Americans have long done best—innovating. A majority of the American public supports action to combat global warming and improve energy security. The next administration should prioritize bringing together the government, private sector, and civil society to discuss next steps to compete in a carbon-constrained world.

SIGNATURE INITIATIVE: INVEST IN A CLEAN ENERGY FUTURE

■ **Establish a Common Principles Charter for Advanced Energy, Security, and Sustainability.** The United States should take a leadership role within international institutions to create a common principles charter outlining sound energy policies and practices that serve as the foundation for global energy security. Provisions of the charter could include protection of sea lanes and critical energy infrastructure; investment-friendly regulatory and legal frameworks that also respect the development needs and sovereign rights of resource holders; regular dialogues between producers and consumers to improve information sharing and facilitate government-industry cooperation; and improved governance and transparency of revenues and sustainability principles.

■ **Create a Level Playing Field to Underpin the Carbon-Constrained Economy.** To expedite the deployment of clean energy technologies, spur the development of new technologies, and create a level playing field on which companies can compete without distorting the effects of subsidies, it is necessary to place an economic value on GHG emissions via a mechanism that sends clear, long-term price signals for industry in all sectors of the economy. The system must be flexible, allow companies to operate around the world, and be integrated into global trade regimes to enable optimal trade of goods and services. There are many mechanisms being proposed to serve as the foundation for this level playing field, and the United States, with its history of creating and maintaining global institutions and norms, must play a leading role in their creation to ensure the long-term stability of any global framework as well as continued global economic stability and development.

■ **Set up and Fund a Joint Technology Development Center.** Energy technology development and deployment are critical elements of any energy and climate solution. International collaboration can play an important role in sharing the cost of and accelerating the pace of innovation. Financial and technical resources, intellectual property rights, and ownership issues continue to remain barriers to greater technology cooperation across borders, inhibiting the transfer of new technologies to developing countries. The U.S. Department of Energy, in partnership with major global energy companies and international and regional development banks, should establish a 10-year endowment for funding energy- and technology-related research. The fund should be administered by an international consortium of the National Science Foundation and its equivalents in large energy-consuming nations and disbursed through a peer-review process to U.S. and international researchers in order to provide venture capital to develop and deploy next generation energy technologies. This could include a special focus on biofuels, which have the potential to play a particular role in aiding development in poor countries.

- Establish Global Free Trade in Energy-efficient Goods and Services. The next administration should negotiate the elimination on a global basis of all barriers to trade and investment in goods and services that contribute to energy efficiency and the reduction of carbon dioxide emissions, along with any barriers to trade in financial services that would inhibit the development of a worldwide market for carbon trading. This could be a first priority for the Free Trade Core in the WTO, as discussed in the previous section.

PART III | RESTORING CONFIDENCE IN GOVERNMENT

Implementing a smart power strategy depends on the government's ability to organize for success. Many Americans, though, have lost faith in government's ability to adapt and work effectively in today's world. They look at the failed health care reform efforts of 1990s, the slow and inadequate response to Hurricane Katrina, the lack of body armor for American troops, and the long lines that plagued our passport centers for a time and wonder what it will take to make our system work again.

Six in ten Americans believe that when something is run by the federal government, it is typically inefficient and wasteful, according to a 2007 Pew poll. This cynicism has led Americans to feel increasingly estranged from their government, with only a third believing that most elected officials actually care what they think. A 2007 Gallup poll revealed that public confidence in the government's ability to handle international problems was at its lowest level since 1972.

This perception of an uncaring, ineffective U.S. government is even more pronounced abroad among non-U.S. citizens. Non-Americans are largely cynical about U.S. motives. In such an environment, difficulties in implementation are often interpreted as malice. Our inability to generate reliable electricity in Iraq is seen as a way for us to maliciously punish Iraqi citizens. The bombing of the Chinese embassy in Belgrade is presumed to be intentional. Any inefficiencies in the visa system or difficulties in entering U.S. territory are assumed to be an American effort to keep certain foreigners out.

Given the low threshold of mutual trust that exists today, it is especially important that U.S. government leaders have the proper mindset, tools,

> "Having a winning strategy is meaningless without the means to implement it."
>
> ANTHONY C. ZINNI

> "Any greater investments in soft power are going to run up against a U.S. military that must be reset and reequipped."
>
> JACK REED

and personnel to implement a smart power strategy. Will the next president be willing to make the hard decisions and trade-offs to put into practice a smart power vision?

There is no silver bullet for ensuring effective implementation of a smart power strategy, and this commission has purposefully sought to stay away from offering sweeping recommendations on government reorganization. Moving boxes around and building new ones is not always the right answer. Even still, the next president ought to undertake a strategic reassessment of government structures and readiness.

Chief among these, the next president is going to face intense pressure to reset the U.S. military, both in terms of manpower and materiel. As this report has argued, maintaining U.S. military power is paramount to any smart power strategy. Although the Pentagon wrestles over the focus of this reset—whether, for instance, it should center on traditional power projection military missions or on future long-duration counterinsurgency or stabilization missions—the president will have a broader set of decisions regarding the proper investments in and balance of hard and soft power tools.

Which tools work and which do not? Which require massive overhaul, and which merely call for new leadership and direction? How can coordination and integration between our military and civilian tools of national power be enhanced?

This chapter seeks to identify some of the challenges that have in the past impeded better integration of our soft and hard power tools and suggests a menu of options that the next president could consider to address this challenge and to maximize effectiveness.

IMPLEMENTATION CHALLENGES

There is widespread understanding that America needs to improve its ability to integrate hard and soft tools into a seamless fabric of capability. There are, however, at least 10 interrelated factors that hinder the U.S. government's ability to bring about this integration.

First, there is little capacity for making trade-offs at the strategic level. The various tools available to the U.S. government are spread among multiple agencies and bureaus. There is no level of government, short of the president himself, where these programs and resources come together. A program in one department, such as English language broadcasting to Pashto-speaking Afghans and Pakistanis, is not easily compared in value against a set of new trucks for an Army battalion. Increasing the size of the Foreign Service would cost less than the price of one C-17 transport aircraft, for instance, yet there are no good ways to assess these trade-offs in our current form of budgeting.

Second, programs promoting soft power lack integration and coordination. The numerous existing programs that promote American soft power—development assistance, humanitarian relief, diplomatic presence, public broadcasting, educational exchanges, and trade—are fractured and spread across many agencies and bureaus. The lack of coordination limits the impact of any of these individual programs and prevents them from being integrated into broader strategies to promote American interests.

Third, the U.S. government has not invested sufficiently in civilian tools. America is increasingly involved in multifaceted tasks such as the reconstruction of states and societies after wars. Yet the civilian agencies of the federal government lack the resources and experience to undertake these complex tasks. By default, the military has had

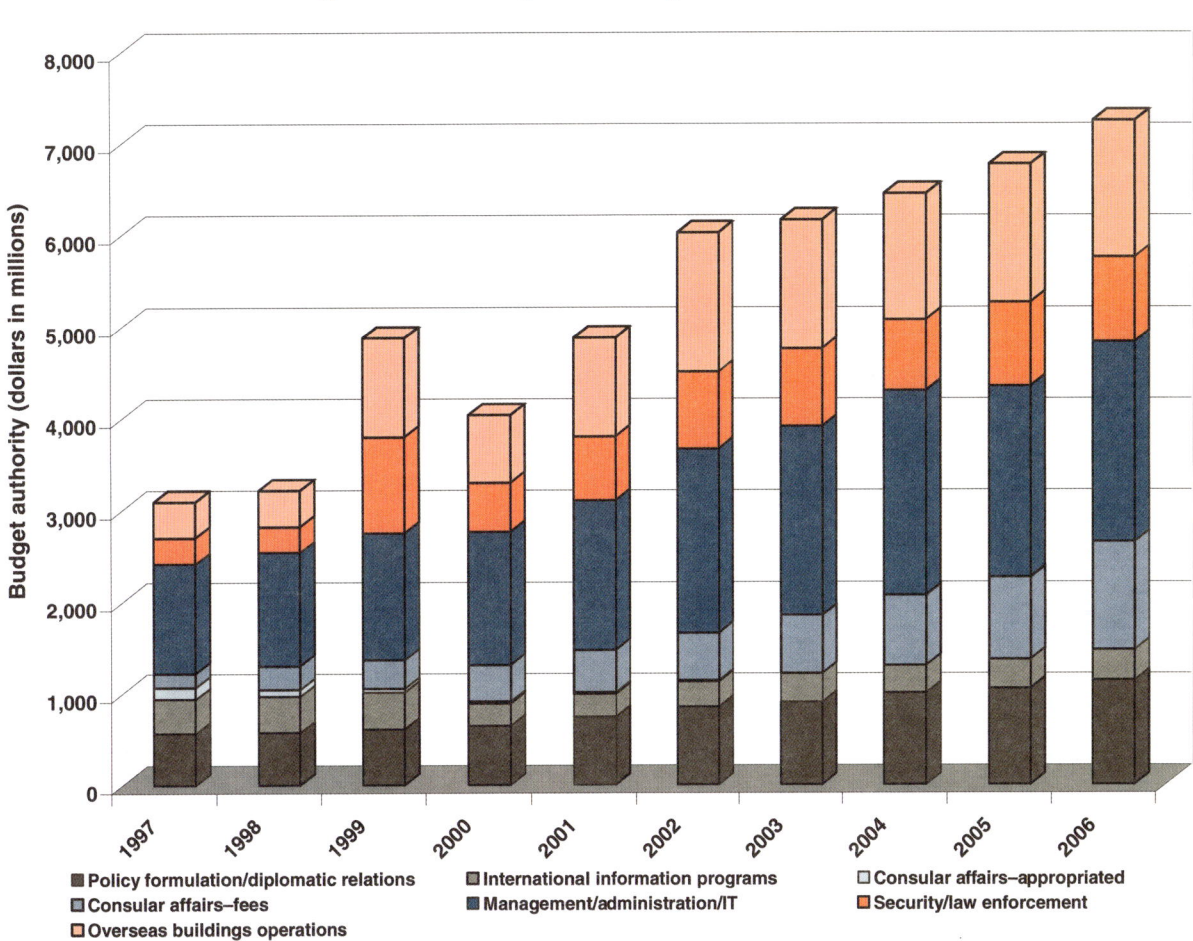

Figure 7. State Department Operations, 1997–2006

Data source: U.S. Department of State, Congressional Budget Justifications, FYs 1999–2008.

to step in to fill voids, even though the work would be better administered by civilian personnel. This ad hoc action by the Defense Department further undercuts the demand that civilian agencies develop these competencies. Figure 7 shows U.S. funding for State Department operations over the past 10 years. Although funding more than doubled during this time, increases were attributable largely to border and diplomatic security activities.

Fourth, civilian agencies have not been staffed or resourced for extraordinary missions. What distinguishes the Defense Department and military organizations is their ability to mobilize resources in times of emergency. The Pentagon is able to respond so ably to crisis because it buys more people in peacetime than are needed for daily peacetime operations. The Defense Department has 10 percent more officers than it has jobs at any one time and uses that extra 10 percent "float" for training exercises and assignments in other agencies. Civilian agencies have not chosen or else not been allowed by Congress to budget a manpower float. As such, they do not have the experience or the depth to take on emergency assignments.

Fifth, diplomacy today requires new methods compared to traditional diplomacy. There was once a time when diplomacy involved American officials meeting quietly to discuss problems with foreign government and private sector elites. Although there is still a central role for these formal channels of dialogue, diplomacy today is far more diverse and challenging. Elites of any one nation today often have more in common with counterparts in other countries than with most citizens in their own country. American diplomats need the capacity to reach beyond these traditional sources of information and channels of influence to better understand and shape views abroad.

Sixth, insufficient authority resides in field organizations. Technology has undercut traditional tools of statecraft. Modern innovations in communications and transport have made it possible for officials stationed in headquarters in Washington, D.C., to increasingly undertake actions that once were only possible by surrogates in the field. The problem this poses is that no headquarters organization can comprehend the complex crosscurrents under way in distant countries. Reform efforts typically place even greater power in the hands of Washington officials, even though a sophisticated understanding of complex local developments would argue for more authority to be vested in field operations rather than less.

Seventh, civilian agencies lack regional operational capabilities. The Defense Department has divided the world into specific regions and given responsibility for all its activities within that region to a regional commander. This permits a region-wide integration of strategies and plans. Civilian agencies lack this intermediate command structure. The Washington headquarters for the civilian departments links directly to a national representative in a given country, oftentimes the country ambassador, who cannot develop regional strategies.

Eighth, short-term exigencies tend to drive out long-term planning. For better or worse, the modern news cycle and the politics of Washington creates disproportionate priorities for addressing near-term crises at the expense of long-term strategic thinking. The National Security Council should be the place for long-term strategic thinking and plan-

> The government must learn to tap into and harness the vast soft power resources in the private sector and civil society.

ning, but it is constantly drawn to breaking crises and urgent developments. This short-term horizon infects all Washington headquarters operations.

Ninth, Congress and the executive branch need a new understanding. Washington politics has become gladiatorial. Cabinet secretaries are pulled before congressional committees in contentious settings. Long-standing congressional leaders of both parties have seen their authority circumvented. A climate of confrontation has displaced a culture of cooperation. This trend has been growing for years, but Congress now puts the smallest directions in law to bind the hands of the executive branch, while the executive branch fails to consult on key national security decisions.

Tenth, many of the tools that promote change are not in the hands of government. The dynamic dimensions of American life today are largely in the private sector, not in government. Nongovernmental organizations, private foundations, businesses, universities, and citizens undertake innovative and exciting activities every day that boost the power and attractiveness of the American model. Vast deposits of soft power reside in the private sector, yet the U.S. government is largely oblivious to these resources and does not know how to tap them for coordinated affect.

TOWARD A NEW APPROACH

The forces of disintegration in our soft and hard power tool kit are strong. It will take a dedicated effort by the next administration to overcome these challenges. In some instances, the problems call for new institutions or renewed mandates for existing institutions. In other instances, the problem can best be addressed with leadership and accountability. Domestic politics and constituencies will also likely shape any reform process. The demands and pressures of America's domestic politics will greatly complicate the development of a sophisticated foreign policy and the investment in tools required to carry it out.

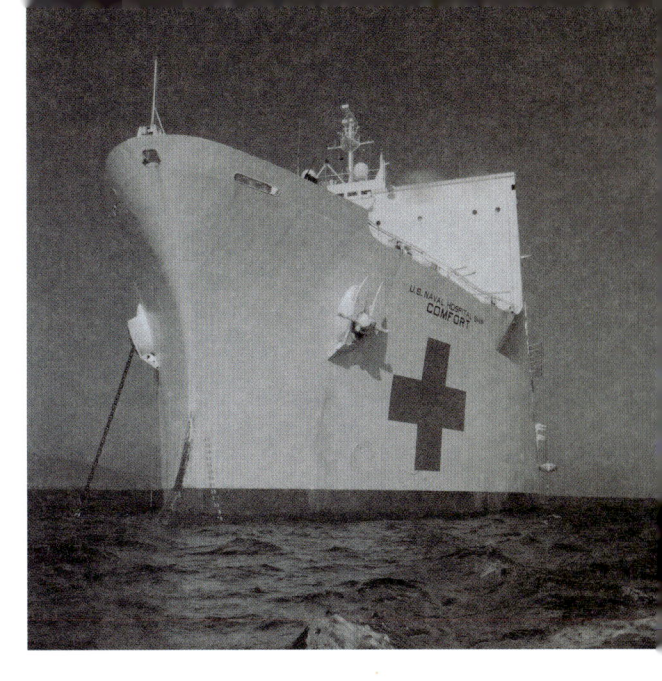

We believe reform is possible, however. We suggest that the next administration should be guided by the following five principles:

1. A smart power strategy requires that we make strategic trade-offs among competing priorities.

2. We must elevate and integrate the unique dimensions of development, diplomacy, and public diplomacy into a unified whole.

3. Congress must act as a partner and develop proper authorizing and appropriating structures to support a smart power strategy.

4. We must move more discretionary authority and resources into field organizations and hold them accountable for results.

5. The government must learn to tap into and harness the vast soft power resources in the private sector and civil society.

The next president and the 111th Congress, both of which will take office in January 2009, will have their own ideas on how to organize for success. However, we offer the following recommendations as a menu of ideas for future policymakers that would support the implementation of a smart power strategy.

> "Eisenhower said that a good organization can't make up for bad leadership, but without a good organization, a leader can't realize his full potential."
>
> CHARLES G. BOYD

Create a smart power deputy. The national security adviser is swept up in the urgent challenges of unfolding crises and lacks the ability to focus on long-term strategy development or manage interagency trade-offs. The next administration should "double-hat" a deputy to the national security adviser and the director of the Office of Management and Budget (OMB), charging this individual with developing and managing a strategic framework for planning policies and allocating resources. This position would have the authority to work with the relevant congressional committees to secure funding for broad strategic purposes.

Add greater coordination capacity to the executive secretariat. It is not widely understood that each major department of the federal government has an organization and an individual designated as the "executive secretary" for that department. The role of these executive secretaries—under the overall lead of the executive secretary in the National Security Council—is to move paper and ideas among the agencies and with the White House. If a planning document is needed for an upcoming meeting of the National Security Council, the executive secretary system ensures that all relevant parties have copies of the document in advance. Although currently this is largely an administrative function, it could be augmented to have larger coordination capabilities. Coordinating the activities of various departments is always a challenge for administrations. There is no existing coordination staff for interagency operations, mainly because there is a policy dispute among cabinet secretaries as to who should be responsible. There is little support for putting a standing coordination staff in the National Security Council because it is not judged wise to have actual operations run out of the White House. The Bush administration attempted to create a coordination capacity to address post-conflict missions with the State Department's Office of the Coordinator for Stabilization and Reconstruction (S/CRS), but its effectiveness in coordinating operations critical to U.S. interests has been limited, in large part because of resistance from existing bureaus, agencies, and departments to "being coordinated." The next administration should consider creating a standing coordination center as an adjunct organization attached to the executive secretary. This option would provide the infrastructure for coordination without having the baggage of bureaucratic turf disputes over departmental roles and missions. This standing coordination organization would be available for use by whichever policy leader is selected by the president to coordinate the federal government's response to a crisis.

Create a cabinet-level voice for global development. As this report previously discussed, there are more than

50 separate, uncoordinated programs administered by the federal government that undertake economic and technical assistance. These programs are fractured, lack coordination, and are not aligned to achieve strategic goals. This represents a major impediment. The next president should task the deputy for smart power to work with the cabinet secretaries to develop a coherent management structure and an institutional plan within the first three months of office. The Bush administration has made important additions to the government's tools through the creation of the Millennium Challenge Corporation and the President's Emergency Program for AIDS Relief. These valuable additions need to be integrated into this coherent new strategy and structure.

Establish a Quadrennial Smart Power Review. The Congress established a requirement in 1996 (H.R. 3230) that the Department of Defense conduct a systematic and comprehensive assessment of its goals, strategies, and plans once every four years. Called the Quadrennial Defense Review (QDR), it has become a major strategic planning process in the Defense Department. The next administration should undertake a parallel process for the civilian tools of national power. The next president should issue an executive order shortly upon taking office that would establish a process and a timeline for this smart power review to parallel the Defense Department's QDR.

Resource a "float" for civilian agencies. As discussed above, the Department of Defense is able to sustain a far superior process for leadership education because it routinely budgets for 10 percent more military officers than there are jobs for them in operational assignments. This "float" permits the military to send its officers to leadership development programs, to work as detailees in other agencies to broaden their professional experiences and judgment, and to meet unforeseen contingencies. Civilian agencies have not budgeted a comparable personnel float. To address these needs for our civilian agencies, the next president should increase the number of Foreign Service personnel serving in the Department of State by more than 1,000 and consider further expansions in other relevant civilian agencies. The value of such an expansion should be considered in the context of comparable hard power expenditures.

Strengthen civilian agency coordination on a regional basis. Civilian government agencies do not have a regional command structure comparable to the Department of Defense. The Defense Department

> Realism and idealism have shaped U.S. foreign policy since the earliest times.

> "Americans are thinking globally and want change. They want to express America's potential for good by providing for others."
>
> FREDERICK D. BARTON

is able to develop region-wide strategic plans because it has regional commanders responsible for large geographical areas. Civilian agencies largely have Washington headquarters operations and single representatives in national capitals. This causes two problems. First, it prevents the development of regional strategies because Washington headquarters operations often get caught up in Washington politics. And second, we fail to get integrated interagency operations in the field on a regional basis. To address this problem, the next president should give the senior State Department ambassadors known as "political advisers" assigned to advise regional military commanders a dual authority to head a regional interagency consultation council comprising representatives from all other federal agencies that have field operations in those regions. Congress and OMB should work to provide the State Department the resources to support these regional coordination councils.

Establish a new institution for international knowledge and communication. U.S. government efforts to communicate with foreign populations often fail to develop thematic messages that resonate due to local distrust and our own misunderstandings of local realities. As a nonprofit, nongovernmental entity, this center would receive federal appropriations to more credibly communicate with populations abroad by tapping into the vast knowledge and intelligence that exist in the private and nonprofit sectors. In particular, it would seek to fill gaps where they exist in four main operational areas: (1) improved understanding (through polling and research); (2) dialogue of ideas (through mutual exchanges); (3) advice to public officials (through expert analysis); and (4) shaping foreign attitudes about the United States to fit with reality (through communications strategies). This new organization would have an independent board comprising notable American opinion leaders with careers inside and outside of government who could provide a "heat shield" from near-term political pressures and would liaise with the numerous federal and private institutions that monitor and evaluate international developments and make recommendations for government action.

A SMARTER, MORE SECURE AMERICA

Realism and idealism have shaped U.S. foreign policy since the earliest times. The very birth of the country occurred when leading citizens in the colonies, upset about taxes and a lack of representation, took up arms and sought to create an ideal form of self-government. America was created as an intellectual pursuit, imbued with great idealism, yet directed toward highly practical goals and objectives. It is simply false to say that some presidents are realists while others are idealists. Every decision in Washington always has elements of both.

It would be similarly false to argue or believe that hard power is shorthand for realism, while soft power is short for idealism. At the outset of the Cold War, President Eisenhower, through the now famous Project Solarium that tasked interagency teams with developing strategies for countering Soviet expansion, concluded that America and the West would not win the global competition with international communism through military means alone.

Military power was needed to counteract the military intimidation of the Soviet Union and the Red Army in Eastern Europe, but the strategy of containment was fundamentally grounded in a political consensus among allies and the dedicated effort to create international norms underpinned by economic liberalism. The dynamism of our economy and free society would win the Cold

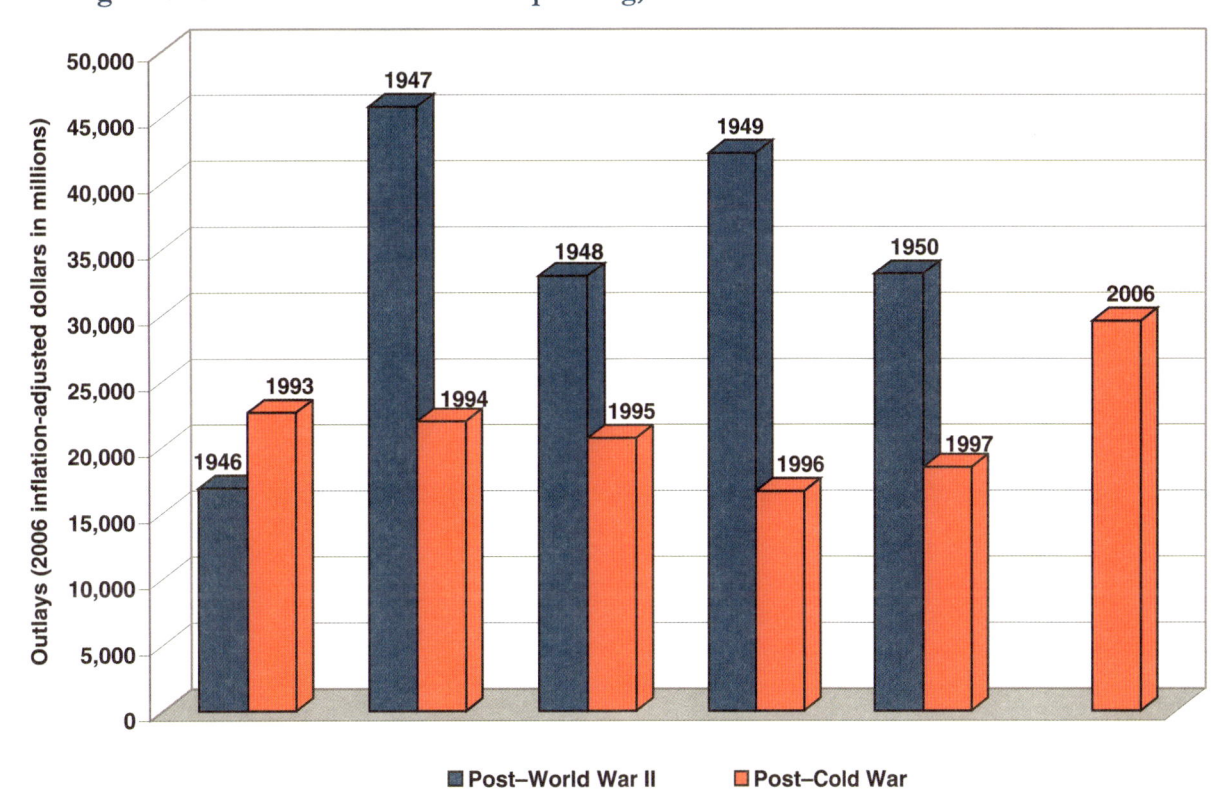

Figure 8. U.S. International Affairs Spending, Post–World War II and Post–Cold War

Data source: U.S. Office of Management and Budget, public database.

War. Figure 8 shows comparable U.S. spending on international affairs at the beginning of the Cold War and in its immediate aftermath. Current investments still do not match post–World War II levels, even though soft power is an essential part of our arsenal.

The business community has a concept, known as "pricing power," that refers to the unique time when a company has a product so desired by customers that the price can be raised without affecting demand. During the first three decades of the Cold War, America held the political equivalent of pricing power. Much of the world admired America and wanted to enshrine American values as the international standard.

Citizens and governments consented to the creation of international institutions and norms that strengthened rule of law, representative and accountable government, open markets, transparent business relations, and support and protection to those who needed help and sought to improve their lot in life.

In recent years our pricing power has diminished. In part this was a product of the ultimate triumph of the West during the Cold War, which left America as the lone superpower. People still admired the idea of America, but felt that our country had become too arrogant and domineering on the world stage.

The terrorist attacks on 9/11 caused America to become a frightened and angry nation. We reacted in ways that alarmed people the world over. We told people in no uncertain terms that they were either with us or against us, presenting too superficial a policy choice for the complex problems we faced. And we relied excessively on hard military power to fight the war against terrorists and violent extremists. Ultimately this is a battle that will be won by ideas, not bullets. Just like the Cold War, we will prevail when the world chooses the opportunities we defend over the despair offered by our enemies.

We understood on a gut level during the Cold War that we could only win with a wide network of allies and with America's leadership in establishing international norms that promoted the peaceful resolution of conflicts, representative governments resolving disputes through diplomacy, an international legal culture of due process and transparency, and economies expanding opportunity at all levels of society. That strategy worked brilliantly in the last century. Today's challenges are different with the rise of non-state actors, but the basic principle that allies and norms extend American influence is just as vital and relevant for this century.

America has all the capacity to be a smart power. It has a social culture of tolerance. It has wonderful universities and colleges. It has an open and free political climate. It has a booming economy. And it has a legacy of idealism that channeled our enormous hard power in ways that the world accepted and wanted. We can become a smart power again. It is the most important mandate for our next president.

APPENDIX

ABOUT THE COMMISSIONERS

Commission Cochairs

Richard L. Armitage has had a distinguished career in public service, most recently as deputy secretary of state (2001–2005). He was also assistant secretary of defense for international security affairs (1983–1989). A decorated Vietnam veteran, Secretary Armitage is president of Armitage International and sits on the CSIS Board of Trustees.

Joseph S. Nye, Jr., is currently a distinguished service professor at Harvard University and a former dean of the Kennedy School of Government. He earlier served as assistant secretary of defense for international security affairs (1994–1995) and chairman of the National Intelligence Council (1993–1994). Dr. Nye sits on the CSIS Board of Trustees.

Commissioners

Nancy Landon Kassebaum Baker (R-KS) represented the state of Kansas in the U.S. Senate from 1978 to 1997. Senator Kassebaum was reelected to her Senate seat in 1984 and 1990, but did not seek reelection in 1996. She is married to former senator Howard Baker (R-TX), who served as U.S. ambassador to Japan.

Frederick D. Barton is a senior adviser and codirector of the Post-Conflict Reconstruction Project at CSIS. He is also a professor at Princeton's Woodrow Wilson School. He was UN deputy high commissioner for refugees in Geneva (1999–2001) and the first director of the Office of Transition Initiatives at the U.S. Agency for International Development (1994–1999).

Charles G. Boyd, U.S. Air Force (Ret.), is president and chief executive officer of Business Executives for National Security. Previously, he served as executive director of the Hart-Rudman National Security Commission. General Boyd enjoyed a long military career and is the only POW from the Vietnam War to achieve four-star rank.

Helene D. Gayle, a medical doctor and public health expert, is president of CARE USA. Previously, Dr. Gayle was the director of the HIV, TB, and reproductive health program for the Bill & Melinda Gates Foundation and had a 20-year career with the Centers for Disease Control and Prevention and in the U.S. Public Health Service, retiring as a rear admiral and assistant surgeon general.

Allan E. Goodman is president and CEO of the Institute of International Education. Dr. Goodman was executive dean and professor at Georgetown's School of Foreign Service. He worked for the directors of Central Intelligence and of the National Foreign Assessment Center under President Carter.

Maurice R. Greenberg is chairman and CEO of C.V. Starr. Mr. Greenberg recently retired as chairman and CEO of the American International Group (AIG) after more than 40 years of leadership, creating the largest insurance company in history.

Chuck Hagel (R-NE), Nebraska's senior U.S. senator, is the second-ranking Republican on the Senate Foreign Relations Committee and also serves on the Banking, Intelligence, and Rules Committees. Prior to the Senate, he had a distinguished career in the private and public sectors. Hagel is a decorated Vietnam veteran.

Sylvia Mathews Burwell is president of the Global Development Program at the Bill & Melinda Gates Foundation. Ms. Mathews Burwell previously served as deputy director of the Office of Management and Budget, deputy chief of staff to the president, and chief of staff to the secretary of the treasury.

Betty McCollum (D-MN) is serving her fourth term in the U.S. House of Representatives representing Minnesota's 4th District. She is also a senior whip within the House Democratic Caucus. Previously, Representative McCollum served in the Minnesota House of Representatives (1993–2000) and taught high school social science.

Sandra Day O'Connor is an American jurist who served as the first female associate justice of the Supreme Court of the United States from 1981 to 2006. She was nominated by President Ronald Reagan. She retired in January 2006 and is currently the only retired associate justice of the Supreme Court.

Thomas R. Pickering is a former under secretary of state for political affairs and holds the personal rank of career ambassador. He is currently vice chairman at Hills & Company and previously worked as senior vice president for international relations at the Boeing Company.

Jack Reed (D-RI), elected in 1996, serves as Rhode Island's senior U.S. senator. Previously, Senator Reed was a three-term member of the U.S. House of Representatives from Rhode Island's 2nd Congressional District. Senator Reed is also a lawyer and a retired U.S. Army captain.

David M. Rubenstein is cofounder and managing director of The Carlyle Group, one of the world's largest private equity firms. A lawyer, Mr. Rubenstein served as chief counsel to the U.S. Senate Judiciary Committee's Subcommittee on Constitutional Amendments (1975–1976) and was deputy assistant to the president for domestic policy (1977–1981).

George Rupp is president of the International Rescue Committee. Previously, Dr. Rupp was president of Columbia University (1993–2002), president of Rice University (1985–1993), and dean of the Harvard Divinity School (1979–1985).

Mac Thornberry (R-TX) has represented the 13th District of Texas in Congress since 1994. Previously, he was deputy assistant secretary of state for legislative affairs under President Reagan. Six months before 9/11, Representative Thornberry introduced the first bill to create a Homeland Security Agency.

Terence A. Todman holds the title of career ambassador. Among his many State Department assignments, he has served as ambassador to Argentina, Denmark, Spain, Costa Rica, Chad, and Guinea; as chargé d'affaires in Togo; and as assistant secretary of state for inter-American affairs.

Anthony C. Zinni is the former commander in chief, U.S. Central Command, in charge of all American troops in the Middle East. A Vietnam War veteran, General Zinni has had a long and distinguished career with the U.S. Marines. He recently coauthored *The Battle for Peace: A Frontline Vision of America's Power and Purpose* (April 2006).

John Zogby is president and CEO of Zogby International, an international polling company. He is also a founding contributor to the Web site, The Huffington Post, and has polled, researched, and consulted for a wide spectrum of business media, government, and political groups.

HOW THE COMMISSION FUNCTIONED

In the fall of 2006, CSIS president and CEO John J. Hamre asked CSIS trustees Richard L. Armitage and Joseph S. Nye, Jr., to chair a Commission on Smart Power that would formulate a more optimistic vision for guiding U.S. foreign policy in the years ahead. The bipartisan commission included 20 national leaders from the government, military, private sector, nongovernmental organizations, and academia. The commission met formally three times to reach its conclusions—in March, July, and September 2007—and engaged informally on a consistent basis with project staff.

The commission was staffed by codirectors Carola McGiffert and Craig Cohen, who served as the principal drafters of this commission report. Their work and the deliberations of the commissioners were informed and guided by a number of important sources who deserve to be recognized here.

Project research was conducted overseas, in Washington, and around the United States. More than 25 CSIS senior scholars (listed on the following pages) lent their deep expertise to the commission by providing regional and issue assessments and writing a set of policy papers to inform the commission's deliberations. Most traveled to their region of expertise to conduct first-person interviews and research specific to the commission's work. CSIS scholars briefed commissioners at the March meeting and commented on drafts of the report. Their work provided the intellectual underpinning of this report.

Three outside advisers—Gordon Adams, Lael Brainard, and Hank Crumpton—briefed the commission at its July meeting on the tough institutional choices facing the next administration. These briefs focused on national security budgeting, development, and counterterrorism. They also made themselves available for personal interviews to project staff throughout deliberations.

A number of CSIS associates and research assistants contributed to the production of this report. Eric Lief, senior associate in the Africa Program, produced all of the report's charts and graphs. Matthew Wills, research associate, served as the invaluable project coordinator for the commission and blog manager. Special thanks go to John Schaus, executive officer to the president, for his good judgment on substance and process throughout, and to Angela Zech who helped to get the project off the ground.

Special recognition is due to Jim Dunton and his publications team, including Donna Spitler Fields, who provided copyediting, and Divina Jocson, who executed graphics work on the charts, as well as Karina Marshall, who produced the beautiful design for the report. We are grateful to the Web team and Bradley Larson for their work setting up the blog. Thanks also go to Mark Irvine for producing the graphics depicting global public opinion. Photographer Liz Lynch deserves our gratitude for many of the outstanding pictures of our commissioners.

In short, the Smart Power Commission project was truly a collaborative cross-center effort, and we are grateful to the full CSIS team who contributed their time and expertise.

Project staff and commissioners were fortunate to have the opportunity to engage informally in off-the-record dialogues with senior members of the media, the diplomatic community, administration officials, congressional staff, presidential advisers, nongovernmental experts, and other opinion leaders to solicit differing perspectives. Eric Ham, CSIS deputy director of external relations, is leading our Hill outreach effort. We are also grateful to the senior staff of our commissioners from Congress who have contributed substantively to this report.

A number of bipartisan research and advocacy organizations also lent their support to the project along the way. These exchanges of ideas have strengthened the report, and we look forward to continued collaboration. Special thanks go to Liz Schrayer of the U.S. Center for Global Engagement and its Impact '08 project, and David Shorr of the Stanley Foundation, both of whom have been important partners. Thanks as well to the Global Development Program at the Hewlett Foundation for insights that improved the commission's final report. We are also grateful to our colleagues at World Learning who served as a terrific resource.

CSIS's "Dialogue with America" played a critical role in informing the commission's work. Smart Power commissioner Rick Barton and project director Karen Meacham traveled the United States and met with Americans of diverse professional and political backgrounds to engage them in a discussion on America's role abroad. These conversations were briefed to the commission and provided qualitative insights into the thinking of Americans outside the beltway. This listening tour was the first major grassroots initiative undertaken by CSIS, a Washington, D.C.-based organization, and its success has helped us to develop a national network of diverse organizations and citizens who are interested in smart power. It is an effort we plan to continue and expand.

In July 2007, CSIS launched its Smart Power Speaker Series, which has brought national leaders not serving on the commission to Washington to discuss America's role in the world in a public forum. Speakers to date have included the head of a Fortune 500 company, a former commander of the U.S. Central Command, a senior adviser to the UN secretary general, among others. The Speaker Series and subsequent outreach efforts seek to make the commission's recommendations an integral part of America's political discourse and will continue throughout 2008.

CSIS has also launched a Smart Power Blog at www.csissmartpower.org. The blog serves as a platform through which CSIS experts can post the analysis they provided to the commissioners, including the results of the Dialogue with America, and comment on the events of the day. The blog provides an easily accessible national forum to discuss U.S. global leadership.

The commission is immensely grateful to the Starr Foundation for making this entire effort possible, and particularly the generous encouragement and support of Commissioner Hank Greenberg. CSIS also wishes to thank the Ford Foundation for its ongoing support of the Dialogue with America; the Rockefeller Brothers Foundation, the Better World Fund, and CG/LA Infrastructure LLC for their support of the Speaker Series.

One of the goals of this project is to inject the concept of smart power into the political discourse, and as such, CSIS outreach efforts will continue well beyond the release of this report. CSIS would like to thank Derek Chollet and Steve Biegun for their advice early in the project on reaching out to the presidential campaigns. Commissioners and CSIS scholars will remain actively involved in briefing smart power ideas and strategy to members of Congress and their staff, presidential candidates and their advisers, other opinion leaders, and the media. It is our hope that the issues explored in this report take on a life of their own outside of CSIS and become embedded in the foreign policy of the next president of the United States.

CSIS CONTRIBUTORS

Project Codirectors

Carola McGiffert
Vice President and Chief of Staff

Craig S. Cohen
Deputy Chief of Staff and Fellow

CSIS Experts

Grant D. Aldonas
William M. Scholl Chair in International Business

Jon B. Alterman
Director and Senior Fellow, Middle East Program

Pierre Chao
Director, Defense Industrial Initiatives
Senior Fellow, International Security Program

Jennifer G. Cooke
Codirector, Africa Program

Reginald Dale
Senior Fellow, Europe Program

Peter DeShazo
Director, Americas Program

Gerald L. Epstein
Senior Fellow, Homeland Security Program

Moana M. Erickson
Deputy Director and Fellow, Scholl Chair in International Business

Steven Flanagan
Senior Vice President and Director, International Security Program

Charles W. Freeman III
Freeman Chair in China Studies

Fariborz Ghadar
Distinguished Scholar

Bates Gill
Former Freeman Chair in China Studies

David Heyman
Director and Senior Fellow, Homeland Security Program

Gerald F. Hyman
Senior Adviser and President, Hills Program on Governance

Sarah O. Ladislaw
Fellow, Energy and National Security Program

Alexander T.J. Lennon
Editor in Chief, The Washington Quarterly
Fellow, International Security Program

Eric Lief
Senior Associate, Africa Program

Sarah E. Mendelson
Director, Human Rights and Security Initiative
Senior Fellow, Russia and Eurasia Program

Johanna Mendelson Forman
Senior Associate

Derek J. Mitchell
Senior Fellow, International Security Program

J. Stephen Morrison
Executive Director, HIV/AIDS Task Force
Codirector, Africa Program

Erik R. Peterson
Senior Vice President, William A. Schreyer Chair in Global Analysis
Director, Global Strategy Institute

Vincent G. Sabathier
Senior Fellow and Director, Human Space Exploration Initiatives

Teresita C. Schaffer
Director, South Asia Program

Julianne Smith
Director and Senior Fellow, Europe Program

Karin von Hippel
Codirector, Post-Conflict Reconstruction Project
Senior Fellow, International Security Program

Sidney Weintraub
William E. Simon Chair in Political Economy

Anne A. Witkowsky
Senior Fellow, Homeland Security Program

Jon Wolfsthal
Senior Fellow, International Security Program

Director, Dialogue with America

Karen Meacham
Visiting Fellow

Research Associates

Matthew Wills
Research Associate
Project Coordinator, Smart Power Commission

John Schaus
Executive Officer to the President

Angela Zech
Former Special Assistant to the Chief of Staff

Research Interns

Adam Ball

Conrey Callahan

Peter Hering

Caroline Kemp

Adam Mirkovich

Sarah Erickson-Muschko

Christine Pirot

Nikhil Tristan Sekharan

Farha Tahir